on track ...
Caravan

every album, every song

Andy Boot

sonicbondpublishing.com

Sonicbond Publishing Limited
www.sonicbondpublishing.co.uk
Email: info@sonicbondpublishing.co.uk

First Published in the United Kingdom 2021
First Published in the United States 2021

British Library Cataloguing in Publication Data:
A Catalogue record for this book is available from the British Library

ISBN 978-1-78952-127-6

Typeset in ITC Garamond & ITC Avant Garde
Printed and bound in England

Graphic design and typesetting: Full Moon Media

on track ...

Caravan

Contents

Where But For Caravan Would I?

Indeed, where would I be? Not writing this, that's for sure. Whether or not that is a good thing is entirely for you to decide, assuming you get to the end of the book.

In the meantime, perhaps a word of explanation as to the hows and whys is in order. Firstly, the hows: how exactly does this work?

The book is divided into four sections. The vast bulk of the text is devoted to what can be termed the canon albums: the studio recordings of original material that are the bedrock on which the band's reputation and history are built. This begins with the *Caravan* album on Verve in 1968 and concludes with the double whammy of 2013's *The Paradise Filter*, to date the last album of original material, and *The Back Catalogue Songs*, 2014's reinvention of the pick of the old tunes. Not something that Caravan haven't tackled before, but the first effort with a settled full band line-up.

Within the canon section, there are some anomalies to this basic idea. *Caravan And The New Symphonia* is a live album but was released at the time of recording (unlike most of the later live releases) and most importantly, it has material that was new at the time of release as well as reworkings of existing songs. *Cool Water* was released nearly twenty years after its recording, but it did consist of new material that was recorded between *Better By Far* and *The Album* and so is obviously part of the canon, although it is discussed at the point of chronological date of release rather than the date of recording. Finally, *All Over You* and *All Over You...Too* are two albums usually included in the compilation sections of discographies as they consist of old songs: this is to ignore the fact these songs are re-recorded and in new arrangements. As such, they can be considered as a canon albums in as much as they show the reconvened band finding their way into a new phase, as represented by subsequent studio albums.

For the Verve and Decca albums, the bulk of the discussion is about the original releases and their running order. Extra tracks have been added to reissues, and these will be mentioned, but mostly they are alternate mixes and edits – attention is given to those tracks that are of note, but in truth the original albums as they played are the canon that fans have grown to love, and for better or worse (any original or thwarted intentions as to running order or tracks omitted aside) they are the canon as we, the listeners, know it, and judge it. These – with perhaps a few exceptions in the categories below – are what really matter.

Live albums and compilations are not discussed in such detail as the studio albums. This is partly to avoid repetition regarding songs, but also because, for the most part, they add little to the Caravan story. There are a few exceptions, and these will merit further discussion. There may be some compilations or live recordings missed – as with all bands of their vintage, there have always been fly-by-night licensees getting product in shops in a 'blink and you miss it' manner. I have tried to include all those that have at least something of interest, no matter how slight.

The BBC recordings are another matter again. In part, this is because the release of these sessions over the years has occurred in a fairly haphazard manner and so needs some clarification; also, because even when there is a supposedly definitive release, it still manages to omit some recordings. Of more import is the way in which these recordings demonstrate another side to the various line-ups that are not always reflected in the canon albums. There are covers, rougher versions of songs that sound semi-improvised in places, and some recordings that show clearly how studio-augmented and arranged pieces could be rearranged to be played as slimmed-down road versions by the band, shorn of extra musicians and arrangements. They can be enlightening and fresh, especially to a listener who has lived with the albums for four decades, yet was just that bit too young to have heard the session broadcasts or seen the band live in their first phase.

Pop and rock meant nothing to me before punk happened. I liked music from movies and TV, some of the classical tunes they played us at primary school, and country and western as the lyrics were stories. Bill Grundy and The Sex Pistols in December 1976 woke me up to the fact that there was something else out there. But the vinyl explosion of punk didn't really happen until the end of 1977. Meanwhile, I had discovered the music press thanks to a third-year secondary school acquaintance in the library (I was a first-year, and all misfits hung out in the library). Of course, that was full of music other than punk. And there was a Harlequin store (soon to be taken over by Our Price) round the corner from the school. By the end of 1977, there was a ton of vinyl being reduced as it was too long-haired, too prog, too weird to sell. I was a fast learner from the music press and had also discovered Alan Freeman, John Peel (not all punk at that stage), and Nicky Horne on Capital Radio. I put names on record sleeves together with loosely associated styles and things I'd heard…

Christmas 1977 saw record tokens and WH Smith tokens, and so it was in the Wood Green branch of Smiths that I bought my first Colosseum II, Peter Hammill, John Martyn and Camel albums. More pertinently, I bought a copy of *Canterbury Tales*, the best of Caravan released by Decca after *Cunning Stunts* (but not including anything from that) as a farewell/cash-in when the band went to Arista. The sleeve, with its faux-Chaucerian parade of musicians and associated Caravan personnel, took my imagination. The brief sleeve note was also the first time I had seen the phrase 'Canterbury scene'. I loved it all, but most of all I loved 'Nine Feet Underground', which I still think has everything that makes Caravan great, and is also one of the first tunes (or 'compendium of several tunes as a through-composed piece', though that's not so snappy) I'd put on a Canterbury Sound primer.

From there, I started to pick up the existing albums wherever I could find them. I was excited by the fact that *Better By Far* was only released the year before, though when I bought it at Easter 1978, the band were in the process of breaking up, reforming twice briefly for *The Album* and *Back To Front* before disappearing for nearly a decade. Those latter two albums were slightly bewildering at the time, as they sounded like the Caravan I was getting to know only in places. As the years have gone by, I understand why, and I have also grown to appreciate those tracks that don't quite fit but are not actually bad in their own right (I freely admit that I don't outright dislike anything the band have recorded, though I do think that some tunes just don't fit in for me, and though good songs may not be 'Caravan' songs).

From here, I became enamoured of the Canterbury sound – assisted no doubt by seeing National Health on *The Old Grey Whistle Test* and then buying their first album – and I still am. Caravan are the poppier, more accessible end of that. No great revelation in saying that, but I do think that this sometimes means they are underrated. What they do as a band is to walk that fine line between a sense of melody and structure that keeps the music easily accessible to even the most casual listener, while also exploring textures, harmonics, melody and counterpoint that can still be challenging and rewarding when listened to closely. In Pye Hastings, they have a songwriter with a grasp of concision, and in Geoffrey Richardson and the Sinclairs in particular, they have had musicians who have had the skill and questing imagination to take the arrangements and playing up a notch when the music demands. At which point I should add that I have always felt Richard Coughlan was an under-valued drummer by Canterbury sound and prog fans as he was not a showy player but rather worked to the demands of the music as a whole. Nonetheless, he has an instantly recognisable style, propulsive and with swing, with fills and rolls that always pushed and prodded at the music, shaping it from the bottom up.

Of course, the wonderful perverseness of most Canterbury sound players is that they have always bristled at there being such a thing. And it would be true to say that there are a lot of bands and musicians who have been co-opted into that style by fans and writers who have no real connection to the geographical area. However, they have been of a like mind and perhaps initially influenced by Canterbury musicians so that the style and feel have become greater than the sum of the parts.

So, what is that sound? In purely musical terms, it's perhaps best described as a compositional style that uses minor keys and chords to create a sense of melancholy, and perhaps at times bleakness. This is relieved by the use of melody that can be bitter-sweet and instrumental voicings in soloing that can be freewheeling and exploratory, creating a sense of release. The cornerstone of this sound comes from The Wilde Flowers, which brings us round to the first Caravan line-up of Pye Hastings (guitar/vocals), Richard Coughlan (drums), and the Sinclair cousins Richard (bass/vocals) and David (keyboards). In essence, Caravan were the last line-up of The Wilde Flowers, who at various times had included the Hopper brothers Brian and Hugh, Robert Wyatt, and Mike Ratledge. Although sounding nothing like the Canterbury Sound as we know it, The Wilde Flowers had been the band in which a group of people who liked soul and jazz as well as beat could come together and start to play. They learned by covering popular songs for dances, jammed out their ideas of what they were listening to in jazz as well as their fledgeling abilities could manage and melded these two together in an embryonic form of the sounds they would later create in various inter-linked combos.

Within this definition, there is a wide range of scope. At one end, you have Steve Miller and Lol Coxhill moving from free jazz into semi-composed areas (neither being from Canterbury, but being pulled in by having known and played with the Sinclairs and Kevin Ayers) and Robert Wyatt's free-form scat singing and the questing playing of Matching Mole; at the other, you have Caravan, who were not averse to soloing or to having some elements that allowed for free and improvised playing, but were more at home with having arrangements to keep these things in check, and never losing sight of the melody and the song structure in what they were doing.

Try as they might, none of these musicians can escape the Canterbury sound as it is rooted in those early Wilde Flowers experiments (see what I did there?). Some, however, were less inclined to experimentation than others. They liked a good tune at the bottom of what they did. Which brings us back again to Caravan: choosing their name, apparently, as they wanted it to represent a travelling caravan of musicians wandering the country and picking up new ideas along the way, they left behind The Wilde Flowers and stepped out of the shadow of previous holders of that name, who were currently touring the States and falling apart for the first time as Soft Machine.

They also lost a bass player – Dave Lawrence – who was plucked from the bunch and discarded for the bloom that was Sinclair R. – who had previously played guitar in an earlier version of the Flowers. And with that, no more flower analogies, I promise.

Ok, so they were really living the life at that point, living as they were in tents during a pauperous summer, but help was on the way. Island ummed and ahhed over a demo tape (allegedly Chris Blackwell asking Pye Hastings who the 'crap singer' was when he called to retrieve the tape, and suggesting they go instrumental), leaving the band hanging on the phone (if there was a payphone near their tents, of course). But never fear – the UK arm of Verve then liked what they heard, and a deal was duly signed...

Here we go!

Caravan (Verve 1968)

Personnel:
Pye Hastings: guitar, vocal
Richard Sinclair: bass, vocal
David Sinclair: organ, piano
Richard Coughlan: drums
Jimmy Hastings: flute
Producer: Tony Cox
Recorded Advision Studios London September 1968; released October 1968
No chart placing.

So, having been signed by Ian Ralfini to the UK arm of MGM/Verve, and having secured a contract with Robbins Music as publishers which ensured a seven quid a week each wage (which was pretty poor even by late 1960s standards), the lads set about recording their first album at Advision Studios in Bond Street under the watchful eye of Tony Cox, who at this time had a reputation forged for his work with Family. And there are those who would place this in the front line of albums that forge the bridge between psychedelia and progressive rock, alongside Family's *Music From A Doll's House*, The Pretty Things' *SF Sorrow*, Traffic's *Mr Fantasy* and Pink Floyd's *Piper At The Gates Of Dawn*.

Really? Where does *Sgt Pepper* fit in, then? It's a bit of an arbitrary list, and although I see the point being made, I think it's a bit of a stretch. This is a very good album, but it's only really an embryonic taste of what was to come. Before we get to the song-by-song, let's discuss this a little.

Caravan, like many bands at this time, had not long stopped being a covers and soul/R'n'B based band with a liking for jazz. They were still finding their way. The songs are credited to the band equally, which may be purely about splitting the publishing and ensuring a wage. The only song that has an extra credit is 'Where But For Caravan Would I?' which has the additional input of Brian Hopper. Interestingly, this is the longest track on the album, and in stretching out, it is one of the tracks that most points the way ahead. The Hopper brothers were always the most jazz-inclined of the Wilde Flowers alumni, as Hugh's subsequent career showed. The songs are basically pop tunes with some flowery arrangements and tasteful playing. I would suspect that the input of Pye Hastings was extremely important here: a man who learned guitar whilst travelling with Kevin Ayers, Hastings was less keen on the soul aspects of the Flowers than other members, and like Ayers was inclined to go for a melody and chord sequence that would be less Stax and Motown, more Vivian Ellis and Noel Coward. Both men had the very rare ability to take elements from the music they had grown up hearing in a pre-rock'n'roll era as well as the music they had then sought out, and fuse that effortlessly into a rural soul music that was possibly what Steve Winwood was seeking, but could never quite find with Traffic (Winwood's jazz and soul influences winning out in his writing).

Now then, here's why I cannot agree with the likes of Nick Saloman (aka the Bevis Frond), a man of taste and erudition in this field of music, who once wrote in *The Ptolemaic Terrascope* that this was, in his opinion, the best Caravan album because of its encapsulation of period and style in a manner that subsequent albums lost in their diffuse playing and influences. It is true that this is a splendid example of that era on the cusp, but when you look at it next to the first Soft Machine album, that has a Kevin Ayers input that mirrors that of Pye Hastings on this album, you can see that the Softs took the pop song and moved it on towards the next landmark by the way they arranged and played. By contrast, the arrangements and playing on this album are more conventional.

There's nothing wrong with that, but for me, that puts this album more on a par with Genesis' *From Genesis To Revelation*: it is a good pop album (thankfully stripped of the arrangements that smothered the Genesis album), and it points the way ahead rather than being a finished article. In the case of Caravan, this may partly be because Tony Cox did not allow them into the mixing (on the pretext that one man doing it would be quicker than five men arguing about it).

And here's an early stab at being controversial by comparing Caravan to Genesis: both bands have, with markedly different commercial results, proscribed a similar career arc.

Eh? Let me explain: Genesis started out wanting to be pop song writers and aiming at the charts. Their early failure saw them turn inwards and become the prog rock band that had subsequent success. The theatrical shows and ornate musical stylings defined what many think of as prog (and was certainly a huge part of what became neo-prog in the '80s revival). They then stripped back the music so that it became more concise and song-based, which saw them scale the '80s and '90s chart heights. As a fan of the earlier music, the production sounds and arrangements of the chart era left me cold, but I could see that this was a natural arc for them to come back round to after their earlier aims. To a lesser degree, Pye Hastings follows this arc as he guides Caravan – consciously or not – through the seventies and into the eighties. The concise song skills of this debut are revisited from *Cunning Stunts* onwards, and with more luck could have seen more commercial success.

In an alternate universe, Caravan from the mid-seventies were the 10cc of their world, with literate, witty pop that garnered the commercial success its quality deserved.

I know what you're thinking: 10cc? Genesis? When are we getting to Caravan's music? Well, we are, in the sense that the subsequent achievements of the band musically are sown here, and also the issues of perception that perhaps have hindered their critical and commercial approbation over the decades. But rest assured, I will mention Genesis only once more (the similarities in construction between 'Supper's Ready' and 'Nine Feet Underground', and why the latter is far superior), and 10cc perhaps a few times (circa *Cunning Stunts* to *The Album*).

Meanwhile, back in 1968, Caravan nearly juddered to a halt before the first album was even released when Hastings was electrocuted at The Marquee, during a support slot to The Gun. Having been thrown across the room by the shock, he was taken to hospital and then advised to go back and carry on (where was Health And Safety when he needed them?), which he was unable to do as the strings on his guitar had melted.

'Place Of My Own' (Hastings/Coughlan/Sinclair/Sinclair)

Still, at least he was around when the record hit the stores. And it was worth his hanging about, as it is a lovely little piece. And the style of the songwriting sets the tone for what is to come from the opening drum roll of 'Place Of My Own', which progresses into a chord sequence and refrain that is pure early Caravan, with Richard Sinclair's voice leading the way (would Chris Blackwell have felt differently if he'd heard Sinclair R, rather than Hastings, on the demo?), and some lovely minor key soloing and trills from Sinclair D. In the first four minutes, you have the next two Caravan albums defined in terms of sound, particularly when Hastings sings the last verse. The switching of voices, the dominance of the organ as the lead instrument, and the manner in which the unobtrusive drumming propels the rhythms.

'Ride' (Hastings/Coughlan/Sinclair/Sinclair)

'Ride' is more conventionally of its time, having a raga guitar line over which Pye sings a winsome melody before it becomes an organ soloing rave-up, which sort of peters out for want of an end. Nice, but sandwiched between the first track and 'Policeman' it doesn't stand out.

'Policeman' (Hastings/Coughlan/Sinclair/Sinclair)

The latter is a piece of music-hall styled humour that is typical of the period but is notable perhaps as being sung and possibly mostly written by Sinclair R – a precursor to the style he developed from 'Golf Girl' onward, and which makes you wish he'd written more frequently.

'Love Song With Flute' (Hastings/Coughlan/Sinclair/Sinclair)

With 'Love Song With Flute' we are getting more to the Caravan we came to know – it begins with off-hand strummed chords and distant singing and develops into an organ-led section that makes space for a gorgeous flute solo from Jimmy Hastings, Pye's older brother (of whom more later), through to the fade. This is four minutes that define the Caravan sound more than anything else on this album.

'Cecil Rons' (Hastings/Coughlan/Sinclair/Sinclair)

'Cecil Rons' is more whimsy, and fits with tunes like 'Neville Thumbcatch' (a la The Attack and – ulp – Peter Wingarde) in that it has mod-pop mixed with a dash of music hall humour. There was an awful lot of this stuff, and much as I have a weakness for this style, this is actually nothing outstanding; it could be any psych-pop band of the era. The coda is more Caravan-ish, mind you.

'Magic Man' (Hastings/Coughlan/Sinclair/Sinclair)

'Magic Man' starts with some nice organ chords leading to a strummed verse and vocal from Sinclair R about doing nothing much that leads into a chorus with Pye Hastings harmonising that sounds like it's going somewhere but doesn't quite get there.

The business of singing about the minutiae of life was a very Canterbury thing, taken to its highest form by Robert Wyatt and hitting an apogee in both Matching Mole and Hatfield And The North, where Wyatt and Sinclair sang about singing. Anyhow, 'Magic Man' fades inconsequentially and we are hit by the strident chords of 'Grandma's Lawn,' with some of the most aggressive playing on the album. That's not saying much, but here they hit the beat and thrust forward in a way that doesn't fit with the rest of the album.

'Grandma's Lawn' (Hastings/Coughlan/Sinclair/Sinclair)

The lyrics seem to be an impressionistic tale of attempted seduction on the aforesaid lawn, but I might be wrong. In a way that wouldn't be seen again for over a decade, this is not a bad song (it's very much of its era), but it's not a 'Caravan' song in execution. Already, we can see that they are so comfortable in certain styles that to step outside that seems to jar. Is this a good thing? It depends how you look at it, but for the confirmed fan, it may be that the jarring elements can spoil an otherwise good record.

'Where But For Caravan Would I?' (Hastings/Coughlan/Sinclair/Sinclair/Hopper)

Finally, we have 'Where But For Caravan Would I?', which is nine minutes, and has definite sections to it and is almost a through composition apart from some refrain. It has space for a meandering solo section early on that has echoes of modal jazz – distant in a guitar/bass/drums/organ pop group, granted, but still there and I would wager the influence of Brian Hopper – before entering an anthemic song section that has some lovely ascending chord sequences and joint vocals before it ends with a riff section that has some extemporising that is not as pronounced as in later recordings, but shows that the ideas for structuring longer pieces were always there, they merely needed to be developed.

It's interesting that Hastings has said that the Hopper credit is due to the melody of the piece being based on something that Brian Hopper had written for the Wilde Flowers, as I wonder which he means – there are three distinct melodic sections, and the first is very slight. I like my theory about the modal section influence, and I'm sticking to it.

Conclusion

Overall, we have a strong if not outstanding debut that shows a band who had a very individual identity but were still developing a musical style that was not heavily influenced by what was around them.

The album was released in mono and stereo. There are occasions when these mixes differ wildly, as some bands used the opportunity to change or add dubbed sections, leading to some different instrumentation or phrasing. This doesn't seem to be the case here as far as I can hear: there is a difference in the balance which means that some sections have a different instrumental emphasis if you listen on headphones, but there is nothing that really makes a great deal of difference. Both mixes were on the reissue CD, so you can make your own comparison with ease.

The original album had a sleeve note by Miles, who was something of a counterculture figure at the time and has also been an ardent historian of the era. But for me, it suffers from his big problem of being too dry, dusty and academic about what was a vibrant era (I prefer Mick Farren on these times, so you can make your own judgements from that). It does, however, make the very pertinent point that Caravan in some ways echo the manner in which Jefferson Airplane were starting to stretch out instrumentally from their song-based roots, and mentions Coltrane's 'sheets of sound' approach to extemporisation, a distant echo of which I would concur is evident in the final track (I can do dry and dusty as well).

Did it do well? No. Did it have a chance? No. MGM/Verve had something of an upheaval at the parent company in the USA, leading to the closure of the London office, leaving Caravan with an album that wasn't available and a contract that was cancelled. Where did our heroes go from here?

Well, they had in the interim gained a manager in Terry King, and through him, were able to get a deal with Decca, that most English of labels, which somehow seemed to suit them. Certainly, what is thought of as their golden era was about to follow for five years and a string of albums that are still fondly thought of nearly half a century later.

CD Reissue extra track:

'Hello, Hello' (single version) (Hastings/Coughlan/Sinclair/Sinclair)
The first thing that Caravan recorded for Decca, however, was included on the reissue of the MGM album (I know, where's the sense in that?), so we'll look at it here. The A-side was a version of 'Hello, Hello' that was different to that on the first Decca album, hence its inclusion (the B-side was the album version of 'If I Could Do It Again…'). There's not a lot of difference in the arrangement, and we'll look at the song in the context of the album. What is immediately noticeable, though, in the difference between this recording and the MGM album is that we have a band who have a stronger sense of identity and more confidence in their performance. It's a brighter band, with a more distinct sound and personality that comes through. The arrangements are slightly more

complex, with some emphases in timing that were not present before, and the range of sounds is greater as Sinclair D adds piano and mellotron to his range, and uses them on this track sparingly but to great effect. The short soloing sections sound different on this recording.

The production is clearer, the band are tighter and have more experience, and they have suddenly made the leap from being one of a bunch of post-psychedelic bands groping for direction into being a fully-fledged progressive* rock band.

(* For the record, there is a distinction between progressive rock and prog rock for me: the former is about any band that took basic rock and tried to move in a direction that defined their own influences and imagination – this could be Black Sabbath, Yes, Fairport Convention, and even later – on those terms – bands like Scritti Politti and Talk Talk that kept moving themselves forward from a rock base; the latter is a defined style that takes much from the Yes/ELP/Genesis style that emphasises technique and ornate composition, and sticks to that as some kind of artistic plateau of quality – there is a lot of good music in that style, but does it really 'progress' beyond that or remain static? Discuss.)

So, leaving that last point on one side, let's carry on.

If I Could Do It All Over Again It Again I'd Do It All Over You (Decca 1970)

Personnel:
Pye Hastings: guitar, vocal
Richard Sinclair: bass, vocal
David Sinclair: organ, piano, harpsichord
Richard Coughlan: drums, percussion
Jimmy Hastings: flute, sax
Producer: Caravan
Recorded Tangerine Studios London, February 1970; released September 1970
No chart placing.

Finding Terry King as a manager was a big step forward for the band. Despite later arguments over money that saw them leave him for the arms of Miles Copeland – only to return for the last leg of their initial run as working band – King's work helped cement their reputation and got them across to Europe where, in common with many of the Canterbury bands, their main audience was to be found and where they were to have an influence that still reverberates in new bands playing those styles.

But no band exists in a vacuum: when we skipped home from the record shop with the latest album and listened to it, poring over every detail, we existed in a vacuum with the music; that's a different matter. For a band to thrive, it needs a network of people who understand where they are coming from and who will support them in the ways they need. That is why they were lucky to fall into the arms of Decca.

Seriously? Decca? The label that spurned The Beatles (infamously, though it was Dick Rowe's assistant who did this, not the A&R head who usually gets the blame)? The label run by Sir Edward Lewis that seemed to completely misunderstand pop to the degree that it was remembered more for Vera Lynn and Mantovani? The label that had brown duster-coated engineers at their West Hampstead Studios and had a staff infamous for in-fighting? A label whose offices I always imagine to be a little like the Ministry offices in the old Launder/Gilliat *St Trinians* films, where pinstripe incompetents complain about no digestives for the tea and try to avoid actually doing anything?

The very same. Why? I'll tell you: while all that was going on, it left some space for a few maverick talents to evolve. Mike Vernon was learning his trade as an engineer and helping Decca quietly become the best label for British produced blues records (by British or visiting US artists) while equally quietly building his own Blue Horizon roster. Vernon's chum Neil Slaven was learning his trade and starting to produce records that moved away from his beloved blues and into newer, more progressive forms; Slaven formed a production company called Gruggy Woof with David Hitchcock, who was working in the art department but harboured a desire to produce, which he later did for Decca, Charisma and others before retraining as an accountant and tackling the finances of Monty Python. It was Hitchcock who saw Caravan and recommended them to his boss, a man who was quietly working within Decca to create an atmosphere where pop could transcend commerce and become something with artistic content that would also reach a wide audience.

Ladies and gentlemen, I give you the unrecognised excellence of Hugh Mendl, a man without whom rock as we progressive-loving music fans know it would probably not have existed; a man who recognised that lasting musical success and worth came from a creative as much as a commercial impulse, and a man for whom I make no apologies in digressing about, as without him there would be no Caravan as we know them. The sum of his achievements is greater than just that, and first, we must stop and acknowledge his career and talent.

Hugh Mendl was an old school gent – public school and university pre-WWII – whose grandfather was on the Decca board. He was interested in music and got a job at the company, working through many departments before war service. Post-war, after a stint as a song plugger, he returned to Decca in a number of capacities. He produced classical and humour albums and a collection of Churchill's speeches. Most importantly, he worked on Lonnie Donegan's early records, and without Donegan, there would be no British rock'n'roll. Mendl had seen the potential of the Beatles and was frustrated at their rejection. He also saw the potential of the Rolling Stones and was instrumental in bringing them to the label. Dick Rowe (obviously keen to redeem himself) took the credit. Mendl was the man who saw John Mayall's Bluesbreakers signed; recognised the embryonic talents of David Bowie and Genesis when presented with them, and most importantly, was behind the formation of the Deram label.

Initially, this was to be a label for new pop sounds: that soon got confused as MOR orchestras trying out the new Deramic Sound System of stereo recording appeared on the label. In passing, Decca had history for this, as their early Phase 4 series of recordings had incredibly complex inserts explaining how the sounds were achieved. All of this was down to how the records were mixed, and this is where Mendl helped changed things for creative bands.

One of the DSS records was to be a version of the Dvorak *New World Symphony* with a pop group playing. The Moody Blues were picked as they were a failing R'n'B band whose hit singles seemed behind them and who had debts to work off. But new boys Justin Lodge and John Hayward had not been part of the hits era and lobbied for the band to throw the blueprint out. So it was that they secretly started to record their new songs, adding the orchestra, having arranger Peter Knight work out new linking sections, and hoping no one would spot them.

They were unlucky to be found out, but lucky it was Mendl, who saw immense potential, trusted them, and quietly closed the door and let them get on with it before lobbying heavily for the release of the finished album: *Days Of Future Passed*. The rest is history.

Mendl saw the Moodies as a huge step forward for how bands thought about their music, and encouraged those of his staff who were forward-thinking to follow the path he had carved out. Hence the ability of Decca and Deram to have some of the best bands of the period. Unfortunately, the other faults of the company remained, which also explains why sales did not always match content, and why Decca as a whole floundered in the seventies. It's also one reason why Caravan, despite having music to match many another 'progressive' band in the era, did not have the commercial impact they deserved.

As for Hugh Mendl – the strain of swimming against the tide caused him to have a heart attack in 1979. When he returned to work, the company had been sold, and his office cleared out. He retired to Devon to run an antique shop, passing away in 2008 at the age of 88. He deserves to be remembered by anyone who likes this kind of music and applauds someone who has the taste and courage to take a leap of faith artistically.

It was worth this diversion as, without Mendl, Caravan may not have gained another contract and faded away as so many did; they may have ended up on a label that killed their career and forced a split after maybe one more album. As it was, they were now on a path that saw them still here, fifty years or more later.

Back at the end of 1969, they decamped to Tangerine Studios in Dalston, where they began work on the new album. The sessions did not go well, and they were abandoned as the band went off on a European tour. When they reconvened in February 1970, they began again. The earlier tracks were later included on the CD reissue of the subsequent album, and with one exception were versions of tunes that were then re-recorded. These will be discussed later. The early recordings also had the take of 'Hello, Hello' that was released as a single and discussed a few pages prior.

The band line-up here remained the same, as it would for the next album, and saw the first real appearance of Pye's brother Jimmy, on sax and flute, after his cameo on the last album. So, this is where we talk about Jim: his contribution to the Caravan sound, especially in the first decade, is immense. Not just because his playing is liberally scattered across the platters, but also because his influence as an older, working musician with a jazz background is writ large on their extended musical palette. Jim is nine years older than Pye, and in that nine years, difference lay work experience that took him through jazz combos in Soho clubs to playing in pit orchestras for musicals. He went on to play with a number of Canterbury Scene alumni as well as Bryan Ferry and a stint of decades with Humphrey Lyttleton. That kind of eclectic experience inevitably rubbed off on his brother and the rest of Caravan. There is an openness in what they played that comes from this: many bands had a defined idea of the sound they were looking for, whereas with Caravan, it seems to evolve in a more organic manner*.

(*I will present more evidence for this theory when discussing *For Girls Who Grow Plump In The Night*, your honour.)

Anyway, Jimmy Hastings is an invaluable member of Caravan in this period, albeit not an 'official' one. This is evident on the album resulting from the reconvened Tangerine sessions, produced by the band with Terry King and engineered by Robin Sylvester (a bassist in bands from the mid-seventies onwards of some note, but here at the start of learning his studio trade).

And so finally to the music!

'If I Could Do It All Over Again, I'd Do It All Over You'
(Hastings/Coughlan/Sinclair/Sinclair)

We begin with the title track, which has become one of their most well-known pieces. Allegedly the title was nicked from Spike Milligan, but it could also be from a Bob Dylan bootleg. Does that matter? Probably not, now: beginning and based around an ascending bassline that breaks into an organ solo that does nothing so much as remind me of the Brian Auger Trinity; it's a simple ditty, in essence, based on a round of the title sung continuously, with a lead vocal over the top that tell of what the singer would do for love. It ends with the round vocal and bass line being stripped back before halting. Frankly, it should have been the A-side of the first single, and things may have been different.

'And I Wish I Were Stoned: Don't Worry' (Hastings/Coughlan/Sinclair/Sinclair)

'And I Wish I Were Stoned: Don't Worry' as a title gives you a fair idea of what the song is about and the feel of the track. Starting with that strummed chord and vocal approach that was a common entry point for Caravan at this point, it develops with a Sinclair R vocal that leads into some organ soloing before recapping the theme, a quick solo with a fuzz organ line, and then into a bridge that takes us into another simple two-chord riff from which they build into a rare guitar solo from Hastings, who generally seems to like being a rhythm player and part of the sound rather than a featured player. A third and different vocal melody builds to the climactic riff.

As can be seen, there is a definite compositional technique at work over these two albums, developing as they progress. Again, all songs are group compositions, and this is obviously at this stage not simply for the publishing split but because they do seem to be knitting together small song ideas each member brings in.

'As I Feel I Die' (Hastings/Coughlan/Sinclair/Sinclair)

'As I Feel I Die' has a lovely impressionistic lyric and musically is wispy and almost silent. Drifting down a river on a sunlit afternoon, watching the dappled sun through the leaves. And then comes a jazzy break from Richard Coughlan that utilises the 'Take Five' Brubeck feel that so many bands at the time adopted to spice up their straight 4/4 timings. Another nice organ solo – how crucial was Sinclair D at this point to the sound?

'With An Ear To The Ground You Can Make It / Martinian / Only Cox / Reprise' (Hastings/Coughlan/Sinclair/Sinclair)

'With An Ear To The Ground You Can Make It / Martinian / Only Cox / Reprise' does the 'beginning quietly then putting the melody into a louder context', then breaks from that to a pointillist marching instrumental break, before we have what I can only describe as the first true Hastings melody line as we came to know them – it vanishes quickly for a long organ solo with some great bass playing underneath from Sinclair R – but for the first time that very distinctive Hastings style emerges. Some lovely flute playing alongside the next song section follows. This is the first time, also, that we see the acknowledgement that these pieces are made of small song fragments in the shape of multiple titles that are full of impenetrable in-jokes and references. It ends with a drawn-out meandering and echoed piano that is quite lovely.

'Hello, Hello' (Hastings/Coughlan/Sinclair/Sinclair)

'Hello, Hello' differs from the original single take in that it has a more laid-back feel, and the instrumentation here is stripped back a little. It's a nagging little bass riff that comes through strongly, and the emphasis is on the organ more than the piano. The lyric about trying to follow a strange little man whose song you can't quite make out is almost Arthur Machen-like before it ends on the piano that is more prevalent on the original take.

'Asforteri' (Hastings/Coughlan/Sinclair/Sinclair)

This is then followed by 'Asforteri', which is a reference to their manager and is a short, pied-piper like round that leads into the defining track of the album...

'Can't Be Long Now / Françoise / For Richard / Warlock' (Hastings/Coughlan/Sinclair/Sinclair)

'Can't be Long Now / Francoise / For Richard / Warlock' is usually referred to just as 'For Richard' and became the central feature of concerts for most of the seventies; 'Nine Feet Underground' aside, it's probably the track by which most fans would define Caravan. Sinclair D was the main composer for this, though the vocal melody came from Sinclair R. It was also the first track recorded on which Jimmy Hastings played. His flute and sax work are integral to this, which begins with a mournful and gentle song featuring empty streets before a drum roll heralds the mighty riff over which the organ solos with melody before breaking off for a tenor sax solo that twists and turns over the bass-propelled riff and some descending and ascending chords. That riff allowed every Caravan keyboard player to let loose, and later for Geoff Richardson to let fly on viola. For now, though, the next chord sequence has tension – where is the resolving chord? – which enables Jimmy Hastings to solo on flute again. The jazzy chord voicings return to build tension before it lays back with more sax. This is purest 'jazz-rock' that Caravan ever recorded, and it's gorgeous. But – and here's the paradox – does it only really sound like 'Caravan' when they pitch into the riff rather than let Jim fly over the top? The return of the fuzzboxed organ to restate themes and propel us into the final riff section answers this, for me: this is defined 'Caravan' character. Crivens, Pye even gets a heavy guitar riff going, over which the organ again plays a solo that is melodic and not just the usual whizz up the keyboard. For me, this is what set them apart from early on: even when stretching out, they thought melodically and not just in terms of fast scales.

There's a reason why this piece came to be such a favourite: it balances melody and riff with enough space for subsequent members to stamp their own character in solos.

'Limits' (Hastings/Coughlan/Sinclair/Sinclair)
'Limits', the end track, fades in for a minute and a half of a slight, jazzy nature that acts almost like a palate cleanser and gentle farewell after such an exhausting ride.

Overall, this is an album that conjures up the kind of summery, rustic feel that the sleeve evokes. The band surrounded by lush greenery, getting it together in the country. Which is not quite true, of course, as the sleeve was photographed in Holland Park, in urban West London. But you wouldn't know that unless you read the small print.

CD Reissue extra tracks:
'A Day In The Life Of Maurice Haylett' (Hastings/Coughlan/Sinclair/Sinclair)
'Why? (And I Wish I Were Stoned)' (Hastings/Coughlan/Sinclair/Sinclair)
'Clipping The 8th (Hello, Hello)' (Hastings/Coughlan/Sinclair/Sinclair)
'As I Feel I Die' (Hastings/Coughlan/Sinclair/Sinclair)

For the reissue, the extra tracks that were earlier takes of album tracks have the same attack as the single version of 'Hello, Hello' and a similar feel of being slightly overloaded in instrumental overdubs. Hastings later remembered this as being everyone wanting to be louder than everyone else (maybe Tony Cox had a point, then?) – whatever the cause, the European tour break straightened that out for them. But we must note 'A Day In The Life Of Maurice Haylett' dedicated to their friend and road manager, which never appeared anywhere else. The lyrics describe exactly that, with soft lines musically punctuated by a crashing snare before breaking into a chord vamp over which the organ cuts loose. The first part sounds like it could be from a stage musical, the second sounds like an instrumental in search of a song. It's nice enough but inconsequential, and it's easy to see why it wasn't re-recorded.

Who needs inconsequential when you have your meisterwerk up your sleeve.

In The Land Of Grey And Pink (Deram 1971)

Personnel:
Pye Hastings: guitar, vocal
Richard Sinclair: bass, vocal
David Sinclair: organ, piano, mellotron
Richard Coughlan: drums, percussion
Jimmy Hastings: flute, sax
John Beecham: trombone
Dave Grinsted: cannon, bell and wind
Producer: David Hitchcock
Recorded Decca and AIR Studios London September 1970-Jan 1971; released April 1971
No chart placing.

Well, here we are at album number three and we have what is considered to be one of the best albums of its era and type, and certainly the album by which the idea of 'Caravan' is defined. You want irony? I got that for you: if Pye Hastings has been the principal songwriter, sole surviving member, and driving force of Caravan for over fifty years, then how do you account for the fact that the album that defines the band for many fans has just one song by him?

Ponder that while we go back to late 1970, and the band retiring to West Hampstead studios in order to begin recording the follow up to their first album for Decca. They had a stable line-up and had a good amount of live work under their belt, which meant that they were a tighter unit, and more in tune than they would ever be again. Add this to the irony list. The man who was responsible for the sound that identified them – an organ style that had moved away from the Brian Auger/Jimmy Smith stylings that most keys players of his generation started from towards a melodic and lyric style that borrowed from the likes of Holst, Elgar and Vaughn Williams – and who would compose half the album and the half that came to 'be' Caravan to many, was about to up sticks and leave.

Not that any of this was in the air when they started to record. As with the previous two albums, the songs were credited to all members equally, but this mostly about the publishing income that allowed them a wage. The truth was that the bulk of the previous two albums had been from the pen of Hastings, who was starting to define the style that took over the Caravan sound. However, the demands of touring meant that there was not much in the locker this time out. With just one song to contribute, it was down to the Sinclair cousins to sort through their backlog of tunes. Richard has never seemed to be the most prolific of writers, but he had three fine tunes which, added to Pye's single offering, gave them a good first side. Cousin Dave, having pondered the way in which the longer pieces on the previous album had been worked out by the band, sat down in his basement flat and wrote several sections which flowed together into one long piece. The window of the flat was nine feet below street level, which explains the overall title of the piece.

21

Production this time was handled by David Hitchcock, who, having got the band onto Decca in the first place by lobbying Hugh Mendl, now finally got the chance to work with them. It's a more robust, less whimsical and flimsy sound than the first Decca album, which works to its credit. After some work in West Hampstead, the band continues at Air Studios in Oxford Street. Sinclair D's long piece, which had not been played by the band before, was recorded in five sections and pieced together by Hitchcock and engineer Dave Grinsted, who did a fine job. The drumming, in particular, is of note as Richard Coughlan's style was to work underneath the music, and he was given a crisp sound that cut through the music to be heard propelling the rhythms but did not overwhelm all around it. It was finally mixed back at Decca and released in April 1971.

Time to put the album on and see what they came up with.

'Golf Girl' (Hastings/Coughlan/Sinclair/Sinclair)

'Golf Girl' kicks off the album with an intro that features a trombone riff. Now there's something you don't hear every day in this kind of music. A jaunty tune with a flute solo, and an organ/mellotron refrain, and a solo on the outro that weaves morse code in and out of the melody, it features some more nifty trombone throughout. A rural tale of encountering a young lady selling tea that leads to something a little more, the cheeky wink of the lyric and the structure of the song was something that Sinclair R returned to later in the decade during his time with Camel ('Down On The Farm'). It's a classic feel-good post-psych tune and is still fresh to me over forty years after I first heard it.

'Winter Wine' (Hastings/Coughlan/Sinclair/Sinclair)

'Winter Wine' follows this, another Sinclair R composition and one which has a more folky feel in the opening and refrain on acoustic guitar and vocal, before the band kick in with a simple propulsive drum pattern from Richard Coughlan that drives it along. The accompaniment is kept simple, the arrangement leaving space for the vocal. This is probably the most vocal-led song that they had recorded to this point. This is good, as it allows us to hear what a lovely voice Sinclair R has: it has the same slightly nasal, wistful and melancholic feel as Robert Wyatt, differentiated only by the lack of the rasp that Wyatt's voice carries. Both are quintessentially English soul singers. The lyric perhaps lets it down a little, being fairly standard stuff for the time and lacking the humour of which Sinclair R was capable and the wit that Hastings always shows. However, when the ubiquitous organ solo kicks in, you can forgive this.

'Love To Love You (And Tonight Pigs Will Fly)' (Hastings/Coughlan/Sinclair/Sinclair)

'Love To Love You (And Tonight Pigs Will Fly)' is the sole Hastings song and is instantly recognisable as such. The rhythm and timing of it are reminiscent of 'If I Could Do It Again...', and it's an example of the kind of witty, literate pop at which he excels. Again, considering that Caravan are a 'progressive' band, the arrangement is very straightforward with only a few flourishes, and some subtle use of mellotron for colour. This was a band who knew when not to play as much as when to play and used that tastefulness to the service of the music. The lyric is one of those 'I'm a naughty lad, but I love you really' lyrics at which Hastings came to excel...

'In The Land Of Grey And Pink' (Hastings/Coughlan/Sinclair/Sinclair)

'In The Land Of Grey And Pink' uses a similar feel to 'Golf Girl', with another humorous lyric that uses a supposed fantasy setting to describe being a village lad in Kent during the youth of Sinclair R. The title itself – which was selected for the album title – comes from an observation made by Sinclair R while looking out over a sunset at Graveney in Kent. It has a lovely little piano solo which prefaces a second chorus organ solo. 'Don't leave your dad in the rain', indeed...

The title and the album sleeve it inspired could be seen as a bit of a problem when looked at in retrospect. 'In The Land Of Grey And Pink' inspired artist Anne Marie Anderson to come up with a village gatefold painting in the appropriate shades that seemed to be full of cottages and houses that grew out of the earth like mushrooms. Everyone who has ever written about it mentions JRR Tolkien, and it does have that feel about it, which is appropriate to the times, but not really what Caravan were about. Because this was their most successful album, both in terms of a musical whole and because of its longevity (it eventually earned them their only silver disc, although it never charted; rarely out of print if at all, 'Nine Feet Underground' was also a staple of FM radio in the early seventies), this image has stuck to an extent, which is misleading and could have been damaging later in the seventies, when the band changed subtly in direction.

'Nine Feet Underground: Nigel Blows A Tune / Love's A Friend / Make It '76 / Dance Of The Seven Paper Hankies / Hold Grandad By The Nose / Honest I Did / Disassociation / 100% Proof' (Hastings/Coughlan/Sinclair/Sinclair)

'Nine Feet Underground' is possibly the best realised long piece of the era for anyone, let alone Caravan. It's through-composed in that there is no theme, statement, extrapolation and then recapitulation of theme, which is how many progressive bands tried to work out long pieces, taking the form from classical music. Neither is it a series of vamps for endless soloing (though there are solos throughout), which was common in jazz-rock bands of the period. What it is, in essence, is nine short pieces and songs, each complete in itself, that run together into one longer piece. And here's where I mention Genesis again (and for probably the last time), as this is also the best way of describing 'Supper's Ready', their magnum opus which was released a year later than this, on 1972's *Foxtrot*. That 'Supper's Ready' is considered a milestone of progressive rock when 'Nine Feet Underground' came first is risible. And bear in mind that I write that while having had my Genesis albums for as long as my Caravan albums. However, while the Genesis track takes seven song fragments which they had and welds them together in a clumsy manner that leads to some jarring contrasts (which sometimes work, to be fair) and has at least one section that seems to have been shoehorned in purely because they had nothing else to bridge the two sections on either side, the Caravan piece is seamless.

'Nigel Blows A Tune' begins with a theme that sets out a chord pattern over which Jimmy Hastings plays a lilting sax solo that is achingly lovely and is one of my two favourite sax solos from a period that had no shortage of great horn playing (the other, for the record, is Dick Heckstall-Smith's in Colosseum's 'Elegy'). It then works its way through a series of titles that are the usual baffling blend of band in-jokes and references ('The Dance Of The Seven Paper Hankies', for instance, is apparently a time-killing game the band, Hitchcock and Grinsted indulged in at West Hampstead), but the titles are irrelevant. The music is all that matters (remember that phrase, I'll return to that in time).

And what music they make: following from the sax solo, we have Pye Hastings singing about the dawning day and a time of hope over a syncopated riff, which then leads into a long, organ-led section where Sinclair D plays some strong melodies and weaves them in and out of the tight band playing. Hastings and Coughlan act as the rhythm section here, while the bass lines start to play counter melodies and in places play against the timing in order to create a wonderful sense of tension in the music. This resolves itself into a section where the tension is maintained by hesitant chords and a sense of windswept desolation, that is broken by a cannon shot which leads into a galloping instrumental section that slows to break down to a reflective piano and vocal section, with Sinclair R reflecting on a quiet place where he can dwell on the past and look to the future (this section is probably the piece of Caravan music that has always affected me most, and this is why I find it hard to be objective about 'Nine Feet Underground' as a whole). The piece ends with a big riff section that has piano and organ winding around the guitar and galloping to an end that resembles a collapsing calliope before a final chaotic chord.

The rest is silence.

Conclusion

So, having produced possibly the best record of the year, success could only beckon, right? Looking back, Dave Sinclair once noted that they had spent so much on recording that the record company gave them no promotional budget, and so the record just crept out rather than was released. Was it this disappointment that led to what happened next? We shall see.

The music should have been all that mattered, and perhaps it is when you're just the listener. But it's never really just about that: consider how important the sleeves were with albums for creating an impression and feel. How bands looked and dressed was as important for so-called image-free bands as it was for pop groups. A progressive band who dressed in three-piece suits and had short hair would have had trouble getting accepted, after all. And if you're a fairly ordinary bunch of hairy blokes, how do you get yourselves noticed amongst other hairy blokes? Daevid Allen pondered this for Gong and decided he liked what Peter Gabriel was doing with a dress and a fox's head, and so Gong adopted colourful costumes to add to their musical mythology. At the time Caravan released this album, Genesis were a year away from *Foxtrot*, and Gabriel was only just beginning to mess around with costumes, noting how the audience reacted. 'Supper's Ready' is a lesser piece than 'Nine Feet Underground', but Pye Hastings didn't put on his mum's evening gown and get the front page of Melody Maker. It wouldn't have suited Caravan to be theatrical, but perhaps there should have been something else? And this is where a decent promotional budget and some ideas around image and presentation should have been discussed. But that never happened.

Meantime, there were some other tracks recorded at the time that only became easily available with the CD reissue.

'I Don't Know Its Name' (Hastings/Coughlan/Sinclair/Sinclair)
The most notable is 'I Don't Know Its Name (aka 'The Word'), which is a Sinclair R song sung beautifully by him. It has a romantic lyric and a slightly sketchy arrangement (saved by some lovely fills from Richard Coughlan). The melody is catchy in places and a bit 'la-la-la' in places, as though this was a work in progress and the top line was never quite completed. It's a pity they didn't work on this a little more, as it's 75% a great song. It has the obligatory organ solo and a nice sax solo from Jimmy Hastings that lifts the mid-section. The organ and piano extended end also suggests that it needed finishing and that this wasn't done.

'It's Likely To Have A Name Next Week' (Hastings/Coughlan/Sinclair/Sinclair)
'It's Likely To Have A Name Next Week' is a demo version of 'Winter Wine' and has an intro that they really should have kept and recorded for the album version, as it has distant, haunting qualities. The demo is worth hearing for some 'I haven't written the lyric yet' scat singing from Sinclair R that is lovely for any fans of his voice. Nice organ solo on this one, too.

'Group Girl' (Hastings/Coughlan/Sinclair/Sinclair)
Similarly, 'Group Girl' is a demo version, with a slightly different lyric, and the trombone replaced by an organ/whistling combo. It's odd to hear, as it's slightly off-kilter in places and shows what a little re-working can do.

'Disassociation / 100% Proof' (Hastings/Coughlan/Sinclair/ Sinclair)

The remix of 'Disassociation / 100% Proof' from 'Nine Feet Underground' seems odd to listen to simply because it's out of context – without the rest of it, it sounds adrift. However, having said that, it is worth a listen because it has some interesting variations on the familiar sections. At the end of Sinclair R's vocal section, there is some additional flute that adds to the haunting refrain, and as this then leads into the final riffathon, you are immediately aware that the guitar sound is very different. No wah edge to it, and it has a sharper, more piercing tone. It also takes a long solo where the released version has an organ solo. It's not bad, actually, and makes you think Hastings should have contributed more leads rather than being so stoically a band player. There's also a bass and drum rumble before the final crescendo. It's refreshing to hear, but to be frank, the unity of the released version makes more sense in context.

'Aristocracy' (Hastings/Coughlan/Sinclair)

Finally, we have the original version of 'Aristocracy', which was re-recorded and released on *Waterloo Lily*, by which time things had changed, as has the timing and rhythm of the song, which here is very much in the style of the rest of their recordings, settling into the same shuffle and timing as the other pieces. It's a really nice version, but the solo here is a bit aimless and wandering, which is a shame as the vocal is good. It peters out as the band just stop, which indicates its demo nature, but here we can see it's of a piece with 'Love To Love You', which it doesn't sound like by the time the next line-up had finished with it.

Ah, yes, personnel changes.

It's worth noting at this early stage that the CD reissue extras were produced by Julian Gordon Hastings, the son of Pye, and someone who has worked closely with his father since the mid-nineties in ensuring not just that the Caravan legacy is maintained but also that the new material the band have recorded is of the highest quality. With Jimmy still around and the Sinclairs maintaining an interest, what a family business the band are!

Waterloo Lily (Deram 1972)

Personnel:
Pye Hastings: guitar, vocal
Richard Sinclair: bass, vocal
Steve Miller: organ, piano, Wurlitzer piano, harpsichord
Richard Coughlan: drums, percussion
Jimmy Hastings: flute
Lol Coxhill: sax
Phil Miller: guitar
Mike Cotton: trumpet
Barry Robinson: oboe
Producer: David Hitchcock
Recorded Tollington Park Studios, London November 1971; released May 1972
No chart placing.

It must have been dispiriting to see all that effort come to very little, really, and to have to carry on as before. It's hard to imagine what it was like being a touring band who were second division in terms of audiences back in the early seventies. If you were starting out, then you had a day job and you put up with the backs of transit vans, no sleep, and no free time as you were working towards turning pro and getting somewhere. If you had a strong selling record and had made it to the big time, then you had the money coming in from touring and sales to, at the very least, prompt your record company to put some cash into decent travel and accommodation. But if you were second division – as Caravan, like so many others, were at this point – then you had the worst of both worlds. You still had the terrible travel and accommodation – and the bad diet that led to, which didn't help the health of many a struggling muso – but at the same time, you had no day job to bolster a dodgy income, as well as the disheartening feeling that you had a deal and a record company behind you - shouldn't it be different now?

David Sinclair must have been plagued by these thoughts, especially as he had put so much effort into what was, after all, a magnum opus. There had to be a way out. He had played some sessions on Robert Wyatt's *End Of An Ear* solo album on CBS after the drummer/vocalist had left Soft Machine, and now he knew that Wyatt was putting together a new band with backing from that label. Matching Mole (a corruption of the French 'machine molle', or 'soft machine'!) had a guitarist in Phil Miller, late of Delivery, and also a bassist in Bill MacCormick, a friend of Wyatt's who had been in Quiet Sun (with Phil Manzanera of Roxy Music, though they did not record any of their set until 1975 when Manzanera's clout got them back into the studio – their drummer was Charles Heyward, later of This Heat and Camberwell Now).

Here's where it gets complicated. Pay close attention in case I get this wrong and you have to correct me.

Phil Miller had been in Delivery with his brother Steve, a keyboard player, and drummer Pip Pyle, who had been a friend since childhood. The band also included singer Carol Grimes, sax player Lol Coxhill, and bassist Roy Babbington. They had been fairly R'n'B based and song-oriented, though not without their jazzier edges. Coxhill was older, a jazz horn man of no little repute as a free player, and had also played in Kevin Ayers' Whole World. Babbington went on to play with Soft Machine and Nucleus. Carol Grimes has had a long career as a blues and jazz singer, solo and in bands. Pip Pyle, after Delivery split, had decamped to France and was in Gong.

Richard Sinclair had met the Millers and had spent some time playing with them. Thus, when cousin Dave joined Phil in Matching Mole, it made sense for him to suggest that Steve join Caravan. Given the freer nature of Matching Mole and the fact that Miller & Coxhill were also by now operating as a duo who played free and also added in some other musicians, it should have set some alarm bells ringing for Messrs Hastings and Coughlan. Although obviously not averse to extemporising, their preference was for more structure and for songs, especially as Hastings' forte was for the latter. Thus the inevitable 'musical differences' were bound to raise their head. A quick listen to the two albums Coxhill & Miller made for Virgin's Caroline label shortly after Steve's brief sojourn in Caravan should make this obvious. They're very good free jazz records, but they have very little in common with what Caravan were doing.

However, the demands of touring and recording wait for no man, and as Hastings later remarked, it was better to have friends you had played with in the band as they could gel more quickly. I can see his point, but perhaps it's not always the best of ideas.

To be honest, momentum is lost both in terms of audience and musically with *Waterloo Lily*. Which is not to say it's a bad album. In places, it's an excellent Caravan album. In those other places, it's also good, but the problem is that it's not really a Caravan album. Richard Sinclair was champing at the bit now that his cousin was gone, and his playing with the Millers had awoken in him a desire to stretch out and start playing in a setting that was less structured and allowed for more free playing. Caravan was never going to be that space.

Before we get to talking about the music on the album, perhaps we should talk about the fallout, as perversely it made Caravan stronger and also opened the door for some excellent music that may not have otherwise come to pass.

Inevitably, the musical tensions evident on the album led to a split, with Steve Miller and Richard Sinclair leaving while Pye Hastings and Richard Coughlan dusted themselves down and carried on. We'll leave them to it for now.

Miller and Sinclair reunited with Phil Miller, who had just left a dissolving Matching Mole, and reformed a version of Delivery, bringing on board Pip Pyle, returned from France. This didn't last long before it became evident a name change was in order to reflect the difference in music, and so they opted to become Hatfield And The North. At which point Steve Miller left, deciding that his muse led him to freer pastures. He formed the duo with Lol Coxhill mentioned earlier, and in fact, an embryonic Hatfields appear on part of the first Miller & Coxhill album. In search of a new keyboard player, they recruited

Dave Sinclair, who of course, had played with Richard before, and with Phil in Matching Mole. Dave Sinclair did not hang about long, and we'll meet him again very shortly. Enter Dave Stewart, ex-Egg and Steve Hillage's Khan (both of whom had recorded for Decca, and Hillage – now in Gong – had been in Egg when they had been called Uriel - are you keeping up? There will be a quiz later). So we had two splendid Hatfield And The North albums before their eventual split and metamorphosis into National Health (incidentally, Jimmy Hastings guested for both bands).

To think that all of this can be said to have sprung from such a troublesome album as *Waterloo Lily*, which was recorded at Decca's Tolllington Park studio by David Hitchcock again. This was November 1971, and it was released the following April. There was less emphasis on the organ this time around, as Miller preferred piano, and so there is a grand piano, electric piano and a Wurlitzer electric piano (which has a unique sound) to add to the sound palette.

The sleeve has a scene for Hogarth's 'Rake's Progress' on the outer, and on the inner a stunning pop art painting in garish colour (as opposed to the chiaroscuro of the Hogarth), and it sets the tone for the opening song, the title track.

'Waterloo Lily' (Hastings, Coughlan, Sinclair)

Immediately, this is a different beast. Sung by Sinclair R and led by a big, bold bass riff, this is a knowing song about ladies of the night and being in the big city. There is some excellent piano and bass interplay and lead guitar – including a solo – from Pye Hastings that shows he can hold his own in this environment. It breaks down for a guest sax appearance from Lol Coxhill that then allows Hastings and Miller to trade over a strident and elastic bassline before returning to the main riff and the song. This is still very structured, but with parts of that which allow more cutting loose than before. It's a harder, tougher, sound with more guitar and not what you might expect. The album's publishing credits are Hastings/Sinclair/Coughlan, with the exception of two pieces credited solely to Miller, but there is little doubt that this first song is mainly a Sinclair R effort.

'Nothing At All' (Hastings, Coughlan, Sinclair) / 'It's Coming Soon' (Miller) / 'Nothing At All (Reprise)' (Hastings, Coughlan, Sinclair)

Next up, we have ten minutes of 'Nothing At All', with Miller's 'It's Coming Soon' sandwiched between. The track fades in with a funk bass riff over which we get some guitar noodling that carries on until Lol Coxhill wanders in and Phil Miller joins the party on second guitar. Now, the thing is that this is actually very pleasant and burbles along nicely before fading, but it doesn't actually go anywhere, which is odd when you're dealing with a band who are strong on themes and melodies. A solo piano fades in and plays a lovely jazzy theme that does have a melody (Miller composed some fine tunes as well as being a good free player). The rest of the band join in for a restrained late-night vamp before a kick drum from Coughlan signals a full band attack on a chord sequence that propels them forward into a long instrumental section that – I swear – sounds like it could have been used for soundtracking an episode of *The Sweeney* (actually, that didn't start until a few years later, so maybe an episode of *Special Branch*, the programme that preceded it), with some cracking bass playing from a man thoroughly enjoying himself, before we return to 'Nothing At All'. Now, this piece is intended to be modelled on Miles Davis' 'Right Off', and tells us much about how Sinclair's jazz interests were driving the band at this point.

'Songs And Signs' (Miller)
Next up is Miller's 'Songs And Signs', which has some great vocals from Hastings and Sinclair singing harmony and against each other. The theme was also used by Miller for 'Chocolate Fields' on one of his Miller & Coxhill albums. Here's a funny thing – this Miller song is so far the most Caravan thing on the album. Work that out. Steve Miller also contributes a lovely piano solo to this tune.

'Aristocracy' (Hastings, Coughlan, Sinclair)
'Aristocracy' starts the old vinyl side two and is a funkier version of the demo song, with a heavier bass sound that powers it along. It's a much stronger version of what is a good Hastings song. Speaking of which…

'The Love In Your Eye / To Catch Me A Brother / Subsultus / Debouchement / Tilbury Kecks' (Hastings, Coughlan, Sinclair)
'The Love in Your Eye / To Catch Me A Brother / Subsultus / Debouchement / Tilbury Kecks' is a return to the tradition of the multi-part song and instrumental cycle and starts with a typical Hastings song which has a guitar solo of melodic brevity before it kicks it a bass-driven instrumental section with a Jimmy Hastings flute solo that sees any jazz inclinations towards free playing kicked into touch, with a well-arranged string section and some brass stabs to punctuate the driving solo. The return of the riff-driven section is altered from previous outings by the guitar being lower in the mix and a long solo section through an effects system that gives the music a sound that is other-worldly and which reeks of riding over the misty Essex and Kent marshes. Is that too fanciful? Maybe, but Caravan's best instrumental sections always paint pictures, and this is no exception. Steve Miller turns in some great piano as part of the rhythm section before stretching out with an echoed Wurlitzer piano section that shows how great he could be as a soloist within a fairly rigid group format. As Hastings takes over the distant wah-sound painting, Miller switches to electric piano to pick up the instrumental theme, run with it, and embellish it with flourishes that are exciting and push the music forward. A brief vocal

refrain and we're into the now traditional riffathon to the finish section, which powers along with piano and guitar shadowing each other while the bass burbles and drives beneath.

As splendid as this is, put against the long track on the first side, it's easy to see that this a band pulling in two different directions.

'The World Is Yours' (Hastings, Coughlan, Sinclair)
The final track, 'The World Is Yours' harks back to 'Love To Love You' in that it has a similar chord sequence and looks forward to the kind of love songs with which Hastings would later fill Caravan albums, but perhaps with less humour and more direct sincerity. It's a touching and succinctly-played tune that is diametrically opposed to the kind of thing that Richard Sinclair and Steve Miller wanted to play.

It's a shame, in a way, as Miller fitted well into the band in terms of his playing, and when they are pulling together, which they are throughout, they are superb. However, it's not how they played together that's the issue: it's what they wanted to play.

CD Reissue extra tracks
'Pye's June Thing' (Hastings)
'Ferdinand' (Hastings, Coughlan, Sinclair)
As far as the CD extras go, 'Pye's June Thing' is just Hastings and acoustic guitar and is another of his love songs. It's a strong tune but seems never to have appeared elsewhere in any form. There's a nice acoustic guitar solo in there, as well. Similarly, 'Ferdinand' is another Hastings and acoustic effort, which this time is one of his songs about a friend who is a bit naughty and leads him astray. Mr Hastings has a liking for end-of-the-pier humour, a bit of double entendre and smut, and some wordplay. In this sense, he fits into the great music hall and variety tradition, with perhaps a touch of cabaret sophistication. This is why I compared him to Noel Coward some time back, and I could also see him plying a songwriting trade at any time, perhaps pre-WWII as a Leslie Sarony or Vivian Ellis style of songwriter. Personally, that's one of the things I like about him. This song appears to have never surfaced elsewhere, by the way.

'Looking Left, Looking Right' (Hastings, Coughlan, Sinclair) / 'Pye's Loop' (Hastings)
The last of the extras is 'Looking Left, Looking Right / Pye's Loop', which is a band performance. It's an unfinished mix but is a great little song that has a jazzy feel but fits into the humorous side of the Caravan song tradition. There's some nice sax and a cracking laid back piano solo. Why they put this to one side and didn't finish it off is beyond me. I would have happily edited 'Nothing At All' down to half its length in order to put this in. It wouldn't have been the strongest track on there, but it would have given the album a more even feel

overall. It meanders out in a series of instrumental rounds that trickle away to nothing before the 'Pye's Loop' section, which is the main riff with some trumpet extemporisation over the top, ending with a telephone ring. It's ok, but I would have faded before the rounds and cut the loop, leaving just under five minutes of actual song. The writer's cut for the album if you will.

Conclusion

So, there we have it: a good band pulling two ways and leaving what sounds like two halves of two good albums, each in search of its mate.

Where could Pye and Richard go from here?

For Girls Who Grow Plump In The Night (Deram 1973)

Personnel:
Pye Hastings: guitar, vocal
Richard Coughlan: drums
David Sinclair: organ, piano, ARP and Davoli synthesisers
John G Perry: bass, vocal
Geoffrey Richardson: viola
Rupert Hine: ARP synthesiser
Jimmy Hastings: flute
Frank Ricotti: percussion
Paul Buckmaster: cello
Henry Lowther: trumpet
Tony Coe: clarinet, tenor sax
Pete King: flute, alto sax
Harry Klein: clarinet, baritone sax
Jill Pryor: voice
Chris Pyne: trombone
Barry Robinson: piccolo
Tom Whittle: clarinet, tenor sax
Orchestra arranged by John Bell and Martyn Ford, conducted by Martyn Ford
Producer: David Hitchcock
Recorded Tollington Park Studios, Chipping Norton Studio and West Hampstead Decca Studios; released October 1973
Did not chart.

With a tour of Australia looming, and perhaps some ground to make up with a fanbase that were slightly bemused by the dual nature of the last album (this in the space of a year, when it took me a couple of decades to really appreciate *Waterloo Lily* warts and all), swift action was imperative. Hastings and Coughlan wasted no time in recruiting Stu Evans on bass and Derek Austin on keyboards. A working four-piece had been put together, but what of adding some other element? With Jimmy Hastings not always available to tour, and the guest players on the previous album having given our ever-present duo a taste for an enlarged line-up, they were on the lookout for something different.

They certainly got that: baffling those that may have expected a horn or wind player, they went and got themselves a string player. And not a violinist, either, of which there were few enough in rock music, but a viola player. Enter a man who is still thought of by some as 'the new boy' (or so he claims): Geoffrey Richardson.

At this time, Richardson had just finished his studies at University, and as a keen musician, had started to make forays into playing live. He knew Martin Cockerham and Barbara Gaskin of Spirogyra, who were just reaching the end of their brief recording career and were residents of Canterbury – the band had originally started as a duo with Cockerham and Mark Francis in their native Bolton, but had decamped south as Cockerham studied at the University of Kent. Despite being in the town, their music had no relation to the infamous (illusory according to Pye Hastings) 'Canterbury sound', being instead more akin to what is now called 'acid folk' for collectors, but is really just acoustic singer-songwriterdom with a dash of trad and some psychedelic influences. Barbara Gaskin was acquainted with some of the musicians thought of as more 'Canterbury sound', and sang on Hatfields and National Health records as well as scoring a number one hit with a remake of Lesley Gore's 'It's My Party' in company with keys whizz and life partner Dave Stewart.

But back then, this was all ahead of her, and in the Caravan story her brief role with Martin Cockerham is pivotal, as they introduced Geoff Richardson to Pye Hastings, and the audition went well enough for a band probably looking for a sax and flute player to recruit a viola player (though to be fair he can play flute as well, and just about anything you put in front of him). The viola was a great choice, by accident or design, as its lower register means that it can swoop in and around the other frequencies in a band with more versatility than a violin, whose high tones consign it within a rock context to being a solo instrument alone. The viola can drop down and act almost as an extra rhythm guitar or double a keyboard line with greater ease. When it is in the hands of a player with a great ear for arrangement and the necessary lack of ego to be part of a band, then it's a positive asset. And Geoff Richardson has a great ear, as his later career as an arranger and session player proved.

This new line-up set off for Australia, and on their return, both Evans and Austin departed. Austin is actually a very good player, who had previous played with Bobby Tench in Gass and with Keef Hartley. He went on to play sessions, work on soundtracks, and to play with Big Jim Sullivan. Along with Evans, they are the forgotten men of Caravan, as they never appeared on album at the time. There were, however, a few tentative sessions that comprise the extras on the CD reissue of the next Caravan album, and on one of these, I think it is easy to see why they didn't quite fit. But more of that anon.

Incidentally, before going any further, let's just dwell on the fact that Geoff Richardson still jokingly refers to himself as 'the new boy'. He's been in Caravan since 1973 and has appeared on more albums than anyone except Pye Hastings and Richard Coughlan. Consider that – he has racked up more studio time and live work than either of the Sinclair cousins, and his playing has been a massive and vital part of the Caravan sound. Without him, every album would sound the lesser, and the one album he did not play on – the original line-up reunion 'Back To Front' – is probably the least, in terms of sonic variety, of any album the band have released.

Where but for Geoffrey would Caravan be?

Well, in 1973, they were bass and keys bereft at the point of starting the next album: where would salvation come from? On the organ and adding synthesiser, we have the return of Dave Sinclair, whose foray into other areas had hit a number of dead ends. Caravan was a steady job - music he knew - and gave him a chance to test his new songwriting partnership with John Murphy. The songwriting was his main focus at this point, but there's nothing like a working band to sharpen the senses. As for the bass slot, Hastings and Coughlan called up John G Perry, who had played in a band named Gringo, with one album under their belt and a support slot on a Caravan tour on their gig sheet. Perry was a bassist with a light touch, nimble and jazzy without being too concerned with stretching out to free playing. He had been playing sessions and working with Rupert Hine, a keyboard player and songwriter who also played sessions and who would appear as a guest player on Perry's first Caravan outing, which had the first of many 'nod and a wink' seaside postcard titles for albums and songs so beloved of Mr Hastings.

Ah yes, I bet you were wondering when I would get to that.

Produced once again by David Hitchcock and recorded mostly at Tollington Park, with some additional recording at Chipping Norton, it was released in October 1973. Hastings firmly seized the reins, writing everything on this release bar one co-write, and steering the band in the direction indicated by the second side of *Waterloo Lily*. Martyn Ford was retained to score and lead the orchestral augmentation, which was sparingly but effectively used.

'Memory Lain, Hugh' / 'Headloss' (Hastings)

It opens with the double-header of 'Memory Lain, Hugh / Headloss', which, apart from its splendidly punning title – something of a Hastings trademark from here on in – has one of the most immediately well-known and recognisable Caravan riffs. Geoff Richardson remembered it as being the first thing Hastings played to him, and he was sold from the off. Rightly so: riffs are always thought of as the bedrock of heavy metal, but in truth, most rock or jazz-based music uses the riff as a hook or basis for a melodic development. Hastings is an unsung king of the riff, as so many initial hooks in Caravan tunes come from his guitar. That his melodic songwriting is the first thing you think of when considering his contribution to the band, then it says a lot about under-rated he has been in this area.

Geoff Richardson is immediately evident from the first few bars, and his playing trades both with that of Sinclair and Hastings; solos and melodic lines pepper the song content as the band stretch out across the first part of the piece before a ringing guitar riff signals the second half, with more trading and swapping lines and some viola playing that stamps Geoff Richardson's identity on the band.

'Hoedown' (Hastings)

'Hoedown' is a short, snappy pop song with some equally snappy viola. It could have been a single and a hit for another band – but Caravan didn't have hits, and Decca were terrible at promoting singles during this period. The title sums up the feel of the song – it's a Caravan 'Saturday night' song if you will.

'Surprise, Surprise' (Hastings)

The following 'Surprise, Surprise' is also just that: the melody is not one of Pye's greatest, as it seems more to be a compendium of his usual melodic twists on the verses, but the chorus is – er – a surprise as it soars with some lovely harmonies. It's also oddly sunny for what is an end-of-the-affair lyric. Perry here shows a deft, light touch with the bass line. It has a splendid viola solo, and it's worth noting that these are already taking up some of the space that previously Dave Sinclair had to fill by himself.

'C'thlu Thlu' (Hastings)

The last track on the vinyl side one is 'C'thlu Thlu', which is either made up by Hastings or a mis-spelling of the eldritch god of foul imagining created by HP Lovecraft and just beginning to creep into popular culture (albeit 35 years after Lovecraft's death). A slow, eerie riff and shared vocals by Hastings and Perry break into a bridge that seems far too jaunty for the alleged subject matter; it's melodically strong before breaking into a section that sounds like the band are soundtracking a cheap horror movie. It's almost like they turn into Atomic Rooster for a couple of minutes, though there's no mistaking the Sinclair style on the keyboard solo.

'The Dog, The Dog, He's At It Again' (Hastings)

Side two starts with a complete contrast and possibly one of their best song cuts. 'The Dog The Dog He's At It Again' is pure Hastings: a 'nod and a wink' title, lyrics ostensibly about a cold but really about getting your lady friend into bed, complete with double-entendre lyrics. This couched in a melody that is embellished by viola lines weaving around the lead vocal and gorgeous harmonies that culminate in a vocal round that spirals upwards and around. All this and a break for a synth solo from Dave built on a great bass riff. To be honest, just for this and 'Memory Lain, Hugh / Headloss', this is one of the great Caravan records.

'Be All Alright / Chance Of A Lifetime' (Hastings)

'Be Alright / Chance Of A Lifetime' is a tune that I know I tend to overlook as it follows 'The Dog, The Dog', but it starts with a great circular riff on guitar and viola, with a Perry lead vocal and some scorching lead playing from Hastings. It prefigures the songwriting style that Hastings would bring to the fore in the Arista years. The hook perhaps lets it down a little before it moves into an acoustic section with Hastings' singing and some winding viola and keys around the vocal melody before a viola solo. Perry gets a chance to shine here, with a splendid counterpointing bassline.

'L'Auberge Du Sanglier / A Hunting We Shall Go / Pengola / Backwards / A Hunting We Shall Go (Reprise)' (Hastings/Perry/ Ratledge)

And so, the final track on the album, which is a tour-de-force. 'L'Auberge Du Sanglier / A Hunting We Shall Go / Pengola / Backwards / A Hunting We Shall Go (reprise)' begins with some delicate acoustic atmospherics before heading into a riff-led section that has some splendid guitar playing before the viola cuts in. There is some very good lead playing on this album as a whole, as if Hastings felt sidelined instrumentally in the last line-up, and although always content to take a back seat before, felt it was time to assert his musical identity, which would also account for the writing domination. Apart from here, where Perry contributes 'Pengola', which is the wistful, orchestrally augmented section with a Davoli synth line from Dave Sinclair (noticeable for its unique sound). It's a mark of how well Perry was chosen that this piece fits seamlessly. The only other non-Hastings write follows – 'Backwards' is a Mike Ratledge composition, and its theme follows equally seamlessly with some dramatic orchestration that builds to lead us back into the final reprise of 'A Hunting...'

This last track is Caravan at their most progressive and shows that they could produce an epic instrumental as well as the next band – except that they didn't have to show off about it, and their solos were perfectly integrated into the music as a whole. But then, prog rock was all about show and artifice, so maybe that was really Caravan's problem: they weren't bothered about that when everyone else was?

Where did they go from here? Blessed with what seemed a stable line-up, they moved forward to producing a concert and subsequent album that utilised their orchestral experimentation to the full, combining new and familiar material.

But back briefly to those CD reissue extras...

'Memory Lain, Hugh / Headloss' (Hastings)

We have a US remix of 'Memory Lain, Hugh / Headloss', which doesn't sound terribly different, to be frank, and is more of a curio than anything else. The rest of the tracks are of much more interest.

'No! ('Be Alright) / Waffle ('Chance of a Lifetime')' (Hastings)

'No – Waffle' is a vocal-free mix of 'Be Alright / Chance Of A Lifetime' and is actually really nice without the vocal – here, the viola that weaves around the vocal line carries the melody and would have made a pleasant piece in and of itself, which can't often be said about backing tracks and says a lot both about the care with which Caravan arranged their material, and also how important the 'new boy' Richardson had already become to the band sound. By chance, Hastings and Coughlan found what they were looking for, and Richardson fell into one of the few (if not the only) working bands that would be perfect for his skills.

'He Who Smelt It Dealt It ('Memory Lain, Hugh')' (Hastings)

'He Who Smelt It Dealt It' (not Hastings at his most subtle) is an early demo version of 'Memory Lain, Hugh' and shows perhaps why the Evans and Austin line-up would not work. The rhythm is slightly slower, clumpier, and the guitars strain to speed up against the beat. Derek Austin's keys are full of organ swells on the accents, and his solo has no real melodic content to it, being about effect and the stabs that add drama to the beat. It's a heavy rock organ solo in a setting that doesn't suit it. He then adds some flourishes that sound leaden against the lighter touches of Dave Sinclair and Steve Miller.

'Surprise, Surprise' (Hastings)
'Surprise, Surprise' is a demo version, with Pye 'doo-doo'-ing his way through the lyric-free melody. Some electric piano from Austin sounds more like it would be at home playing on the test card. Does that sound harsh? Probably, but as with the previous take, he's a keys player in the wrong band. He later played for Sheena Easton, and that kind of MOR pop piano is what he's playing here.

'Derek's Long Thing' (Hastings/Coughlan/Richardson/Austin/ Evans)
But it's the eleven minutes of 'Derek's Long Thing' that are the real proof. Starting with some great portentous piano, and with some splendid ominous and snarling Hammond playing as it progresses, it's a really fine prog rock instrumental, perhaps in search of a vocal, and certainly an influence on 'Cthlu Thlu' on the album made after his departure, but it really has more in common with Atomic Rooster than Caravan. Hastings and Coughlan were never going to become a hard rock band, and that was where Derek Austin was going with this. Pye still turns in a good solo, as does Geoff, and they sound like a band enjoying playing the tune, but *Waterloo Lily* had already taken that pulling in opposing directions vibe. It couldn't happen again if the band were to prosper.

Caravan And The New Symphonia (Deram 1974)

Personnel:
Pye Hastings: guitar, vocal
Richard Coughlan: drums
David Sinclair: organ, piano, synthesiser
John G Perry: bass, vocal
Geoffrey Richardson: viola
Lisa Strike, Vicki Brown, Margot Newman, Helen Chappelle, Tony Burrows, Robert
Lindop, Danny Street: backing vocals
The New Symphonia conducted by Martyn Ford
Producer: David Hitchcock
Recorded by the Pye Mobile at the Theatre Royal Drury Lane October 1973;
released April 1974
Did not chart.

Original Album run order:
'Introduction' (Jeffes)
'Mirror For The Day' (Hastings)
'The Love in Your Eye' (Hastings/Coughlan/Sinclair)
'Virgin On The Ridiculous' (Hastings)
'For Richard' (Hastings/Coughlan/Sinclair/Sinclair)

CD Reissue version run order:
'Introduction' (by Alan Black)
'Memory Lain, Hugh / Headloss' (Hastings)
'The Dog, The Dog He's At It Again' (Hastings)
'Hoedown' (Hastings)
'Introduction' (Jeffes)
'The Love In Your Eye' (Hastings/Coughlan/Sinclair)
'Mirror For The Day' (Hastings)
'Virgin On The Ridiculous' (Hastings)
'For Richard' (Hastings/Coughlan/Sinclair/Sinclair)
'A Hunting We Shall Go' (Hastings/Perry/Ratledge)

This album was the culmination of a project headed by John G Perry and
Martyn Ford, produced once again by Hitchcock and re-mixed from the live
recordings at Air Studios, to pull together the New Symphonia for a one-off gig
at the Theatre Royal in Drury Lane London, on the night of 28 October 1973.
For Girls had only just been released earlier in the month, and this could be
seen as by way of promotion as well as a next step on. To record it and put
it out as an album was an obvious move, given how expensive it would have
been to mount even the shortest tour with such an entourage.

But why do this? Caravan were still outside the first division in terms of sales,
despite a solid fan base and some decent press. They hadn't broken through

with one killer album or freak hit single, like most other bands they were lumped in with as progressive. Soft Machine themselves, possibly the premier Canterbury band, had been forced to trim their horn section back to just Elton Dean a couple of years earlier because touring costs were prohibitive. And did it add anything artistically to what the band were trying to do?

Well, I think the answer to that is in the affirmative. They had used orchestral augmentation over the last two albums to great effect, and so the idea of enlarging their sound palette further must have been appealing. Look at it this way: there were many types of progressive band. Some wanted to dig deep into their sound and refine the instrumentation they had to a greater whole; some wanted to expand their instrumental technique and tackle more difficult pieces of music; and some wished to explore new sounds, be it conventional or more avant-garde. Caravan fitted into the last of those categories, and although certainly not avant-garde, the notion of new sounds had always been of interest. Their music was based around composition and songwriting, so therefore the idea that they would want to adapt existing pieces to show off their technique or that they would want to look to covering work from outside their idiom to prove their virtuosity, was anathema.

The Caravan way was to take extra instrumentalists and bring them into the overall picture, using them on some already existing compositions, and also writing some new material specifically with the idea of working with the orchestral canvas to paint new sound pictures.

A very noble and interesting aim, and the perfect time to do it: the idea of progressive rock was at its height, and by the time the album was released the following April, the well was running dry: the excess of both the top line progressive acts and the heavier bands who were selling in large numbers, plus the slow demise of chart pop into the drudgery of formula, meant that many were already starting to wonder if there was something a little more rootsy that was available. Pub rock and then punk were seeded in the discontent of Emerson Lake And Palmer and Led Zeppelin reaching their most bloated. Even something as tasteful as a band playing in harmony with an orchestra on some extended instrumental pieces that focused on melody and harmony would not be tolerated. This is possibly why this is, in many senses, the most progressive rock album that Caravan would make, before the songs began to take precedence and Hastings and Coughlan steered the band towards more pop-oriented waters (albeit bloody clever and witty pop).

The original album consisted of four Caravan tracks, of which two were new, one revisited their first orchestrated piece, and one was a reworking of the live stalwart For Richard'. They were preceded by an introductory piece written especially for the evening by Simon Jeffes. A musician, composer and arranger of no little flair and imagination, Jeffes was shortly to launch his concept of the Penguin Café Orchestra on the public. In this, different musics and styles were played and welded together in new and interesting forms, always with an accent on melodic content. Jeffes' work here is an insight into this and is also of note as he would have met Geoff Richardson, who later went to be a part of the Penguin Café Orchestra and work on projects with Jeffes until his untimely death. Such is the lure of the Café, however, that Jeffes' son took up the baton and continued the work.

However, the original album gave a slightly distorted view of the evening by picking out mostly new work, an older tune, and one perennial crowd-pleaser: the actual running order of the evening was markedly different, with a large chunk of the just-released *For Girls* also played on the evening, and there's a very good reason it was not used on the album beyond the fact it would duplicate material within a year. 'Memory Lain, Hugh / Headloss', 'The Dog, The Dog, He's At It Again' and 'Hoedown' preceded the Jeffes' piece, which was a prelude to the suite of new material, their initial orchestral experiment, the inevitable 'For Richard', and then concluded by an encore reading of 'A Hunting We Shall Go'.

The CD reissue of the album is not so much a reissue with extra material as a proper outing for the whole concert in the correct order. It adds a good 35 minutes to the original 43 and puts everything in the right order. Which, of course, makes it hard to assess: for decades, Caravan fans lived with the original album, but should we look at it as it was for the concert-goers that evening? For me, you have to look at the original and then put it in the context of the second issue (which is, in effect, what this is, rather than a reissue). So that's how we'll do it, and then look at what the second issue brings to the table.

'Introduction' (Jeffes)

The original album begins with an orchestral flourish and comic sound effects that bring to mind the kind of musical humour Gerald Hoffnung was responsible for in the 1950s and sets up a mood that is then punctuated by the band coming in for a chord sequence with viola overlay. The orchestra fades in, the band fades out and we get a light music climax before the band come back for a viola solo. As the chord sequence climbs, the orchestra punctuate. There is no melody as such, but a theme that suddenly dies in an orchestral spiral.

'Mirror For The Day' (Hastings)

So, following that introduction, we fade the orchestra into 'Mirror For The Day', descending strings underpinned by guitar and the vocal. The backing vocalists are sweet behind Hasting's voice, and the band have an ascending riff to compensate for where you expect the chorus to be. No matter, as the chorus comes in where you expect the next verse, but the structure doesn't seem at all cock-eyed. The band have a stronger presence here, the orchestration being used to accent and punctuate.

'The Love in Your Eye' (Hastings/Coughlan/Sinclair)

'The Love In Your Eye' follows, and the orchestral accompaniment here is filled out considerably from the version on *Waterloo Lily*. It's also a lighter and less grounded version of the tune, as Perry's bass is nothing like the driving style Richard Sinclair used. This takes a great chunk out of the frequencies in the middle and at the bottom end of the sound, giving the orchestral textures a chance to be heard. Dave Sinclair contributes a splendid solo that highlights the difference between his style and that of Steve Miller, while the section about halfway through breaks down to allow Perry to cut in and around an extemporisation on viola. The orchestra takes over a riff previously played on keyboard and add dramatic emphasis to the final vocal section before the final riff section, for which the orchestra allows the band to rock out with a Hastings solo and growling fuzz bass from Perry.

'Virgin On The Ridiculous' (Hastings)
After this, 'Virgin On The Ridiculous' is a complete contrast, with a sweet and sweeping orchestral backdrop for one of Hastings' sublime love songs, with a rousing chorus augmented by the backing vocalists' harmonies and a sawing viola that leads to a breakdown with oboe and guitar, woodwinds, and then a galloping instrumental section with a keyboard solo that is punctuated by percussive volleys. This slows to a final anthemic verse from Hastings and a valedictory melodic passage on keyboards with the theme echoed and played around the band by the orchestra. It is a stunning melding of band and orchestra, and one that even when I am in two minds about the album, works perfectly.

'For Richard' (Hastings/Coughlan/Sinclair/Sinclair)
And so, the concert came to an end (encore aside) with the orchestrated 'For Richard', which begins with the strummed chords and Richardson's viola augmented by the orchestra, with an arrangement that plays with harmonic constructions that set up a questioning atmosphere into which the vocals cut in suddenly. The strings blend with the viola until Richard Coughlan kicks in, and the orchestration drops back to allow Richardson and Perry to kick on for the next section. It's easy to forget how important Perry was at this point, as his playing is strong but never overpowering and nimble enough for his four strings to compete with those of the viola. As we move into the riff section, Sinclair takes over the solo melodic role while the orchestra plays the riff, the brass particularly effective in taking the guitar section. As the keys solo progresses, the strings and brass swirl around, counterpoint and harmonise with the band, leading up to the crescendo that climaxes that section of the piece before dropping back to allow Richardson and Sinclair to play off each other, adding string riffs that are unobtrusive but lend colour to the background. The winds cut in for a jumping, bouncing counterpoint to the rhythm, brass added for effect as the time changes again, before it moves back into a keyboard-led section that leads up to the final changes. Here, the orchestra comes in and shadow the riff, punctuating the beat with colours that take the piece to a widescreen canvas. Sound like I'm getting carried away? It's

hard not to when you listen to this again. Part of you may want the viola, guitar and keys to trade off each other without interruption, but the fact is that by backing off and allowing the orchestration to bring these colours, they turn the piece from a delightful miniature to a large canvas on the gallery wall.

Additional Tracks On The Reissue

Okay, so I am getting carried away: but that was the original release. How did the enlarged version, the full concert, change the perspective on this?

'Introduction' (by Alan Black)
'Memory Lain, Hugh / Headloss' (Hastings)
'The Dog, The Dog He's At It Again' (Hastings)
'Hoedown' (Hastings)

Well, the first surprise, of course, is that the first three tracks, from the then-current album, are played as a kind of hors d'oeuvre by the band. The rather irritating Alan Black introduces the night, explains how it came about, and then describes the first part as a 'warm-up' and a 'featurette'. The band then come on and charge into 'Memory Lain, Hugh / Headloss' at a rapid clip, showing what a great live sound they had at this time. It's a good performance with Richardson's viola leading the charge. The good Mr Hastings then introduces 'The Dog, The Dog...' with the explanation of how it's about a flasher running out of the medication that stops him running off to Hampstead Heath in his long mac, before they play the song without the massed harmonies of the studio, but with Perry and Hastings manfully trying to make up for that with just the two of them and somehow pulling it off. The solo section enables Dave Sinclair to bugger about on the synth before finding his melodic sense at the last moment and saving the solo. Unable to reproduce the massed harmonies at the end, the baton is passed to Geoff Richardson to deliver a fine melodic solo which is ably supported by more nimble playing from Perry, emphasising how well these two had gelled in the line-up. The first part of the concert ends with a speedy dash through 'Hoedown', which has a middle breakdown for some more viola – er – fiddling which builds with the guitar towards the last chorus.

'A Hunting We Shall Go' (Hastings/Perry/Ratledge)

From here, we progress into the original album as already discussed and then round things off with the evening's final track from *For Girls*, 'A Hunting We Shall Go', which this time is played with the orchestra. I know this is nit-picking as the original album showcased the orchestral project, which was the point of the evening, but doesn't it strike you as perverse that the orchestra did not play on the *For Girls* tracks at the beginning of the evening on which orchestration was used in the studio? Weren't those scores available for at least some of the orchestra to play? Or was that a cost thing again? Having said that, this is a bravura performance from the band, and on this final track, they kick off beautifully until the orchestra come in from about the four-and-a-half-minute mark when things slow down for the 'Pengola' and 'Backwards' sections of the piece, which feature a lengthy and melodically delicate organ solo from Dave Sinclair which the orchestra weave around with great care. As we move into the reprise of 'A Hunting...' the band kick up a notch before a wash of white noise and it's all over. And so, the 'reissue', or complete concert finally (however you wish to think of it), comes to an end.

Conclusion

So, ultimately the question is this: was it a successful experiment? For me, the answer is a reserved yes, with the proviso that the reservation is completely subjective. The band make space in their playing for the orchestra, and when I am in a receptive mood, I think it works, and it adds a lot to the feel of the music. But there are times when I just want to hear the band play a little more, as they do on the first three tracks of the reissue, and I feel that the orchestra can't make up for the interplay that they had as a five-piece. But if I want that, I can go back and listen to *For Girls* or just the tracks on the second issue to hear this line-up. It says a lot about their confidence as a band and as musicians that, at this point, they felt they could allow an orchestra space without being overwhelmed by them or without trying to blast them away. I have deliberately avoided mentioning other bands with orchestras simply because those I have heard, always – to me – fall into either of those categories. Not so here, which is a triumph.

Just as well, as it was about to be all change once again.

Cunning Stunts (Deram 1975)

Personnel:
Pye Hastings: guitar, vocal
Richard Coughlan: drums
Mike Wedgewood: bass, congas, vocal, Moog brass, string arrangements
David Sinclair: keyboards, string and brass arrangements
Geoffrey Richardson: viola, flutes, night-shift whistle
Jimmy Hastings: brass arrangements
Producer: David Hitchcock
Recorded Tollington Park Studios and West Hampstead Decca Studios September 1974-May 1975; released July 1975
Highest hart placings UK:50, USA:124

Caravan were never the most stable of bands in line-up terms, but at least they had tempered that with a consistency in label and management. That was all about to change, as with this album, they terminated their relationship with both Decca and with Terry King. They also had yet another line-up change in the bass department and chose to use this album to start their shift away from what could broadly be termed 'progressive' rock and towards a more song-based style that would see them fit better in the company of 10cc than Yes. All the while producing what for me is their most consistent – and best – album since *In The Land Of Grey And Pink*. Had their style changed that much since then? In some ways, no: they still had three of the same musicians and composers in the band, but the whimsy had been toned down, and the style sharpened so that there was less extended soloing and purely instrumental passages: now, those skills were put to the service of the song form.

I realise that this may be contentious, as there are probably a number of long term fans who view them as a 'Canterbury sound' prog band and mentally lump them in with the likes of Soft Machine and the Hatfields. They share common ground, it's true, but as Pye Hastings assumed overall control (even if he only became captain of the ship, with Richard Coughlan as first mate, simply because they never quit like everyone else), so his instinct as a songwriter guided their direction.

Having said that, on this album, the writing is shared out between the band in measures that only give him about a third of the album's credits: but who said he couldn't be paradoxical?

The shift in musical direction was slight, but the choice of replacement bassist when John G Perry left is indicative of intent. Perry had been playing sessions the whole time he was in the band and was also working with Rupert Hine on a studio-based band named Quantum Jump, which also included drummer Trevor Morais, whose credentials were long established in sessions and from his days in The Peddlars. A melodic jazz, funk and rock outfit who were primarily instrumental, they eventually had a hit a few years after the fact with 'The Lone Ranger', by which time Hine was also producing and utilising his mates on sessions. Perry was a busy man, and Caravan were not the band to make him rich, for many reasons. Between Gringo (whose tour support had brought him to Hastings' attention) and Caravan, he had also recorded with Spreadeagle, and two failing bands plus one with money issues gave him pause for thought. His departure, however, seems to have been amicable as his solo album included guest shots from Caravan members. He also toured with Gordon Giltrap and Aviator before settling to sessions and library music for a career.

Enter the somewhat unlikely figure of Mike Wedgewood as new bass in town. An interesting choice, given that his career so far had jumped from one end of the spectrum to the other. He had played bass in Curved Air for a while (where the drummer at the time was one Stewart Copeland, which may have been significant as his brother Miles was also their manager), and most recently had been the bass player and musical director for Kiki Dee, who was a fine singer in search of a direction, and who had been looking in a distinct chart pop direction and away from her soul roots. Wedgewood was a bass player with a more upfront, driving style than Perry, which gave the rhythm section more bottom end and propulsion than on the last two albums, and he knew his way around a studio. More importantly, in the context of his joining, he was also a songwriter with a strong grasp of melody and arrangement. His recruitment was a statement of intent: this was a band wanting to move out of the 'cult' band section and garner a wider audience. Moreover, this was a band who knew they had the ability to do this and the necessary skill set (after all, much as I adore Van Der Graaf Generator, the idea that their skills would be suited to such a shift is risible).

For many a band, this kind of change would be concern enough, but for Caravan there were other, more pressing concerns. Their management deal with Terry King was causing them money issues that were eating at the heart of the band. As soon as this album was completed, and before it was toured, Dave Sinclair had departed again. Not, this time, for musical reasons, but because of issues with money. The accounting was causing dissent and argument, and the questions were: 1. Where was all the money going, as they didn't seem to be seeing too much return? 2. Was King really worth his percentage? The early title 'Asforteri' was originally 'Asforteri25', as he was on 25% of the band's earnings. That had been fine when they first signed to Decca but had he really built them a career since then; were the negotiations on new contracts really working to their advantage; and where was the push for promotion?

This last query indicates where the band were at with the record company. Decca were a fine label for allowing bands to develop and grow and not terminating contracts for one stiffed album. The influence of Hugh Mendl was massively important in this regard. But he was forever fighting an uphill battle, as were any bands who had long-term contracts. The Moody Blues had continued their successful run, and Camel had arrived after one failed MCA album to grow to a point where they could play the Albert Hall with *The Snow*

Goose; but most bands with long-term deals merely burbled along, at the mercy of the office infighting and the seeming inability of the label to get it together for their pop/rock acts. John Tracey, who ran the reissue programme in the late 1980s through to the millennium, began at Decca as an office boy and was responsible for picking out several novelty and one-off hits for the pop division as his opinion – as 'a youngster' – was sought. Sir Edward Lewis, who still oversaw the company, relied on a long-standing employee who had started as a lift operator and would tell the old boy what he thought he wanted to hear. The idea of Decca, and what it had been, was wonderful – but it hadn't moved with the times and was also hopelessly disorganised in the pop division. It had been for some time – can it really be true that the only reason Egg's *The Polite Force* was released was because no-one realised they were in the West Hampstead studio recording it until it was almost finished, believing their contract had been terminated after the first album?

If Caravan were to reach that next level, this had to be their last album for Decca. They needed a label with more get up and go, so they could be got up and gone. And for that they needed a new manager, who might just help them get some money back at the same time.

With all this going on, it's astounding that they produced such a great album. Even more astounding that it was the first Caravan album to actually chart in the UK, just cracking the top 50. In the USA, it reached 124 in the Billboard pop chart – that may not sound very high, but it was triumph for a band seen as FM radio college fodder. There was much to build on here, and when you listen to the album, it's not hard to see why. Produced once more by David Hitchcock at Air, Tollington Park and West Hampstead between heavy touring, it shows a band at the top of their game. Jimmy Hastings guests once more, and there is once again the use of an orchestra on two tracks – but significantly, this is less the classical-influenced arrangements of the last two albums, but something that is much more in a pop and light music vein, heralding their new intent.

The title, however, is another matter. It was originally going to be called 'Toys In The Attic', after a phrase for going mad that an American friend of theirs used. Hastings, in particular, was not keen on this, and it must have been with some relief that the change was forced by Aerosmith getting in there first with an album under that name. And so, a last-minute substitute to change the game... Another of the band's little jokes, it's a Spoonerism that comes from a Richard Coughlan joke: what is the difference between a magic wand and a policeman's truncheon? One is used for cunning stunts; the other is for stunning cunts!

'The Show Of Our Lives' (Sinclair/Murphy)

The record itself, on the other hand, is a thing of beauty and sentiment, particularly on side one. Piano chords fade in with an immediately effective swooping and simple bass line from Wedgewood. 'The Show Of Our Lives' was the first time Sinclair's writing with John Murphy had made an appearance, and it's a very straightforward and memorable melody with a strong vocal and lyric and some good harmonies. It also has Wedgewood singing lead, which shows both how good his voice was, and also how well he fitted into the Caravan sound. The fade-out of 'ring the bells and sing' in a crescendo of vocals, church bells and guitar is superb, but the masterstroke here – and throughout the next couple of albums – is the lead guitar. Why Hastings, having shown his worth, was content to drop back to strictly rhythm, is open to question. However, the promotion of Geoff Richardson to lead guitarist was inspired: he plays his lead lines as he would on a viola, leading to a lyrical and sustained melodic style that would flourish over the next few albums.

'Stuck In A Hole' (Hastings)
'Stuck In A Hole' is a Hastings tune with a cracking pop melody, cowbell, and a great hook. It has 'hit single' written all over it and was released as one. Of course, being Decca, it flopped - still, it does have some splendid viola flourishes and a strong synth solo across the middle eight. This is Hastings' songwriting condensed into three minutes, though with a lyric that for once eschews jokiness.

'Lover' (Wedgewood)
'Lover' is Mike Wedgewood's first writing credit, with a lead vocal from him that is underpinned by his bass and Sinclair's piano, along with a string section that swells and grows through the track. It's not the usual kind of Caravan song, but they make it theirs, especially where the bass and guitar carry a melodic line that is less solo than theme, leading into the second half of the song, which eventually builds into a climax where the string section and band repeat and play against themselves, building up a wall of sound that is based on one simple but affecting riff while Richardson's viola plays over the top.

'No Backstage Pass' (Hastings)
The strings segue into 'No Backstage Pass,' wherein Hastings proves he can do lovelorn ballads with strings just as well as Wedgewood, but with his own distinctive melodic style. The use of the string section here ties the two songs together nicely and bridge the styles. The odd lyrical twist is typically Hastings, and there's a good guitar solo where Wedgewood's bass riff cuts in on the choruses and drives the tune along, upping the tempo towards the end, which sets up the end of side one nicely for the second Wedgewood tune.

'Welcome The Day' (Wedgewood)
'Welcome The Day' is uptempo, with more of a funk feel to the driving bass and drums, while Richardson weaves viola around another Wedgewood lead vocal. Interesting to note this: Hastings may have been the ship's captain, but once again, he shows how content he is to take a backseat for the good of the

music. He does take over the lead guitar here for a fine solo before a synth solo from Sinclair weaves around the funk riff.

So, side one is a great pop record. Side two could have put that out of balance, as it's given over almost entirely to Sinclair and Murphy's 'The Dabsong Conshirtoe', complete with the usual jokey titles as six parts take up the next eighteen minutes. Was this another attempt at 'Nine Feet Underground?'

'Dabsong Conshirtoe: The Mad Dabsong / Ben Karratt Rides Again / Pro's and Con's / Wraiks And Ladders / Sneaking Out The Bare Quare / All Sorts Of Unmentionable Things' (Sinclair/ Murphy)

Most assuredly not. This is more akin to six songs and pieces that link together and are segued, rather than being a through composed piece. Being of Sinclair's collaboration with Murphy, they are much more focused on strong vocal melody, and although there is a lot of instrumental interplay and some passages are of instrumental-led melody, the emphasis is on the vocal sections. Lyrically, it harks back to 'Waterloo Lily' in that it appears to chart a young man's progress from innocence and love into a world of sin and decadence and his attempts to come to terms with that. Starting with a sweet acoustic melody, it moves into a section where the band kick into gear, from Hastings to Wedgewood on vocals, and then into a section that could be a successor to 'Waterloo Lily' about ladies of the night, with a climbing chord sequence, and some synth and viola interplay. Moving into a church organ section that is representative of a great revelation, a melancholic melody with flute fluttering around breaks down to a jazzy chord sequence over which Jimmy Hastings contributes a flute solo of typical tunefulness before a jazz piano excursion from Sinclair is followed by mellow jazz guitar from the Montgomery school shadowed by synth. And we're only just over halfway through at this point.

Richardson's viola picks up the theme, horn punctuate the arrangement, we move back to the original flute line before an ominous chord leads us into the riff section, wherein Hasting's wah-wahs his way through the riff and instrumental stabs bleed in a sound collage of noises, dubs of previous sections, atonal chords and voices. Nightmarish, and perhaps indicative of our young hero's confusion and awakening. Perhaps more 'Candide' than 'Rake's Progress'? It ends with a sudden reprise of the fade from 'The Show Of Our Lives', which somehow makes perfect sense. Honestly.

'The Fear And Loathing In Tollington Park Rag' (Richardson)

As a palate-cleanser, perhaps, we finish the album with 'The Fear And Loathing In Tollington Park Rag', a first composition from Geoff Richardson, which is a sweet minute and a half of guitar rag with a rising bank of violas that bring it to an all-too-brief climax.

A great album, worthy of the progress it saw the band make. The reissue has three extra tracks.

'Stuck In A Hole' (single edit) (Hastings)
The first is the single edit of 'Stuck In A Hole', which frankly sounds no
different to me…

'Keeping Back My Love' (Hastings)
The next track is perhaps more of note. 'Keeping Back My Love' is a Hastings
song that didn't make the cut. It's strong enough, but there was so much
material already for side one that it would have unbalanced the timing for
cutting if placed there (anything over 22 minutes reduced fidelity when cutting
for vinyl as it squeezed the grooves too close together), and it would have
sounded out of place tacked to side two. This is a shame, as it's a fine pop
– almost power-pop – tune, with a cracking lyric and a good, tight viola and
synth solo. A dynamic performance, it shows up the re-recording of the song
(with a new lyric) as 'Behind You', on *Better By Far* and is indicative of the
issues that album faced.

'For Richard' (Hastings/Coughlan/Sinclair/Sinclair)
The third extra is a live version of 'For Richard', which was recorded at the
Fairfield Halls, Croydon, on Mike Wedgewood's first gig. For any thoughts on
this, refer to the listing for the *Canterbury Tales* compilation as that was its first
appearance chronologically and where I first heard it. As it was pivotal to my
growing love of the band, any thoughts are best recorded there.

Meanwhile, back in 1975, change was afoot (again).

Blind Dog At St Dunstans (Arista 1976)

Personnel:
Pye Hastings: guitar, vocal
Mike Wedgewood: bass, vocal, congas
Jan Schelhaas: keyboards
Geoffrey Richardson: viola, guitar, flute, night-shift whistle
Richard Coughlan: drums
Jimmy Hastings: flute, saxophone, clarinet
The Chanter Sisters: backing vocals
Producer: David Hitchcock
Recorded Graveney Village Hall on the Manor Mobile; released April 1976;
Highest chart placing UK:53

By the time the last album was released, David Sinclair had departed because of those money issues and was starting up a band with John Murphy on guitar and Richard Sinclair on bass. At the risk of sounding flippant, you could see that it wouldn't last too long before one or either of them decided to leave. The Sinclairs, for all the talent they have and however much I have loved what they have done over the last half century, have proved themselves to be bolters: when the going gets tough, or even when it just gets a bit boring, they get restless feet and are off before you can say 'turn that amp down'. So, it's no surprise that this band did not last long, although David and John Murphy kept writing together. The next public sighting of the Sinclairs was about three years later when they both turned up in Camel. Richard arrived first for *Raindances* and *Breathless*, then they played together live, but by the time of *I Can See Your House From Here,* both had departed. Funnily enough, the second keyboardist on that tour was a man who is about to enter the Caravan story.

Jan Schelhaas is not, despite the name, a Dutchman. I say this as for years, at least some fans (alright, just me) got his prior history confused with Ton Scherpenzeel, who replaced him in Camel. Ton was in Kayak, the Dutch progressive band. Jan, on the other hand, had been in The National Head Band and with Gary Moore circa his *Grinding Stone* era before playing sessions with the likes of Thin Lizzy. And he's from Liverpool. Not that this is important, it's just that I would like to be clear on this. And also on the fact that his joining Caravan was another piece in the transition towards clever pop rather than progressive rock: Schelhaas is an adept keys player, but at this time favoured piano and synth rather than organ, so there were less lengthy keyboard solos on this and the next album, with an emphasis on short and sweet fills and breaks. If you like, the George Harrison approach to a solo: a quick break on the chorus and let's get to the middle eight.

Musically this is important, as this album was the one that would hopefully push them further into the mainstream. I'm biased, as this is one of my two favourite Caravan albums (along with *Grey And Pink*), but let me state my case, as it has often been written that this record was detrimental to their career. It wasn't: it was more successful in terms of chart placings. Musically, it distils the instrumental stylings that had distinguished the band and places them in the context of melodic songs with witty (sometimes coarsely humorous, but funny is funny, right?) lyrics, wrapped around Hasting's guitar riffs which were now placed as hooks at the beginnings of songs rather than the bedrock of instrumental excursions.

No, what was detrimental to their career were the prevailing winds – about which they could do nothing – and some misjudgements in the face of those winds. But that was to follow. Right now, they were on the cusp of a new beginning, and not just musically. Terry King and Decca were consigned to the dustbin of history (albeit only temporarily in the case of the former), and there was a new kid in town managerially.

Miles Copeland was the son of a CIA operative who had been brought up in the Middle East and North Africa. His mother was a Scot who worked in British Intelligence. This made him perfect for the jungle of the music business. He started BTM (British Talent Management) in 1974, managing Renaissance and Curved Air, where his brother was the drummer, alongside one Mike Wedgewood. Miles' other brother Ian was a concert booker. What wasn't to like? Copeland promised great things, as he was obviously highly skilled. He was also prone to over-reach himself at this stage, which was to be fatal for Caravan within the next two years. Right now, in 1975, he was a Godsend.

Through his BTM label (a division of his company), Caravan found themselves on Arista, still a fairly new label and the baby of Clive Davis, who was a star-maker and had a nose for the commercial. Which was what his label promoted and so was unlikely for the old, progressive Caravan, but just what the new, thinking-person's-pop group Caravan needed.

With David Hitchcock still in the production chair, and Jimmy Hastings adding clarinet to his flute and sax duties, the band now decamped to Graveney Village Hall (the same village from which Richard Sinclair had once viewed a sunset over 'the land of grey and pink') with the Manor Mobile studio to record the new album, mixing it in the familiar surroundings of Air Studios. They were on top form playing-wise, as Jan Schelhaas had survived a baptism of fire coming at the last minute for the *Cunning Stunts* tour and even getting through a live TV concert (released many years later, as you will see in the live albums section).

In terms of songwriting, this was the Hastings show, with all bar one of the compositions being from his pen. Mike Wedgewood got one song only this time around, though it is the second-best song on there and makes you wish for more from him.

The title comes from something Noel Coward said when a child asked him what two rutting dogs were about: 'the doggie in front is blind, and the one behind is pushing him all the way to St Dunstans,' Not only does this tie in with my own personal theory about Hastings and Coward, but it also has band resonance: St Dunstan is the patron Saint of Canterbury, and the cartoon on the sleeve is of St Dunstan's Street, near the old West Gate of Canterbury. There are pubs along there that were very familiar to Caravan members past and present. The sleeve itself is worthy of comment as it's a detailed and amusing cartoon which shows a suavely dressed blind dog, complete with cigarette holder, standing in the road while around him anthropomorphic dogs crowd the street as they go about their business, with a number of dog-related jokes. A traffic warden argues with the driver of a Rover; the hot dog seller is selling 'hot humans" there is a signpost to the Isle Of Dogs and Yapping (Epping) Forest; there is a Barkely's Bank, a travel agent advertising the Costa Del Battersea, and a bus numbered K9; a crowd of laughing dogs watch a dog throwing a bucket of water over two humans on a tandem; there is also a woman carrying a book called 'A Hunting We Will Go'... On the reverse, cartoon representations of the band gather around the blind dog as he sits in a cane chair, holding a brandy glass while Schelhaas offers him a light.

It's worth noting all that simply because the sleeve is an important tool for the album: it sets up their essential Englishness, their sense of humour, and is good-natured, denoting that this is not a 'serious', furrowed-brow kind of record, but one to be enjoyed. The production echoes this as it is bright and dynamic, capturing some good performances of strong songs.

'Here Am I' (Hastings)
'Here Am I' is a statement of intent from the title on. Starting with a flourish of crashed chords and synth arpeggios, it moves into a tale of a man looking at the world and wanting things to get better, underpinned by the bass before a gentler verse with viola takes us to a guitar break from Hastings that roams melodically over the chord sequence of the verses and then into the dynamic chorus and a reprise of those initial chords. Another verse, and then a breakdown to gentle chords and the viola lamenting across them. A final valedictory verse and then fade.

'Chiefs And Indians' (Wedgewood)
'Chiefs And Indians' is Wedgewood's sole credit and vocal. A piano refrain and a tale of a man who doesn't want to be the one to argue and wants to save his relationship – to a piano and viola refrain. The band come in with a guitar theme from Richardson, which gives Wedgewood the chance to discuss the title lyrically with some great '20s jazz clarinet punctuation from Jimmy Hastings before a section where guitar, electric piano and synth get to shine before we go back to the vocal. The initial piano line fades in for a reprise of the initial melodic section before the song drifts away on the breeze.

'A Very Smelly, Grubby Little Oik / Bobbing Wide / Come On Back / Oik (Reprise)' (Hastings)
'A Very Smelly, Grubby Little Oik' kicks off the medley that also comprises 'Bobbing Wide' and 'Oik (Reprise)' with a great riff that hooks you into the

song, which has a lyric about a little bloke with foul habits who is nonetheless a charmer. It moves into a synth solo from Schelhaas, which gives him a chance to stretch out a little. There are recurring riffs and themes in here that hook as much as the vocal chorus and take us to a Richardson guitar solo and a chorus that hits a high note that is sustained across a slower flute-led section for 'Bobbing Wide' before leading into 'Come On Back', the vocal of which is Hastings switching from humour to sentiment over an easy jazz rhythm while Schelhaas decorates the song with some splendid lounge piano before the straighter tempo of the chorus. Switching between the two, the song progresses to the final chorus, with more jazz clarinet, before this segues into the 'Oik (Reprise)' section, which ends up breaking down into chaos, with the Chanter Sisters singing the lyrics. Backing vocalists of some repute in the era, their voices grace many a release, but perhaps never one with a lyric like this...

'Jack And Jill' (Hastings)
'Jack And Jill', which kicks off side two on the old vinyl, begins with a road-digger of a bass riff which powers the song along, with some syncopated guitar and viola lines. It's based on the old nursery rhyme, but in this retelling of it, the good Mr Hastings is in the role of Jack, and his Jill promises to reward him if he brings her some water. Know what I mean? I think you do. It's Hastings at his splendid end-of-the-pier nudge-and-a-wink best lyrically, and it's interspersed with a burst of viola to spice up the sound. The bass riff is repeated in a breakdown, and it's an interesting change of approach in terms of the arrangement, allowing a concise organ break from Schelhaas before, as in all great songs of this music-hall style, our man has his intentions thwarted, along with what sounds like a locked groove on vinyl (had me looking when I first bought it) followed by a spoken section with flowery flute while an old man explains the blind dog line to a questioning child.

'Can You Hear Me?' (Hastings)
After that, which is quite unusual for Caravan in arrangement and shows that they could still go for something new, we're back on familiar ground with 'Can You Hear Me?' which is another riff-hook and sweetly melodic vocal melody from Hastings, this one taken at a fairly fast pace with a viola solo and some organ flourishes around the guitar hook. It then takes a left turn to slow down with a root bass note and slower tempo that allows for the viola to lament like some old Scots air to the fade. On paper, that shouldn't work, but in the context of the song, no matter how odd it may seem, it sounds glorious as it leads out the last 45 seconds.

'All The Way (With John Wayne's Single-Handed Liberation Of Paris)' (Hastings)
'All The Way (With John Wayne's Single-Handed Liberation Of Paris)' is, despite the subtitle, one of Hastings' best romantic ballads and one of my

favourite songs of all time. It also sounds very like the kind of soft pop that Radio 2 would have played during the period. Middle of the road, which were dangerous words for a rock band in those days, and could spell the death of any credibility. But who cares, when you have a song that opens with a lush synth refrain before gentle chords and a heartfelt lyric about finding the person you wish to spend your life with are delivered with a flute drifting around the lines. The chorus builds in ascending chords with sawing violas bolstering the sound, preceded by a soft sax solo. As the chorus carries on, flute plays over the top. At nearly nine minutes, it's too long for a single, probably too long for radio play on the kind of stations that should have played it, but then again, it could have been edited. It fades away to a man (Geoff Richardson) whistling the refrain as he disappears into the distance.

You won't get anything remotely approaching objectivity from me about this song, as I love it, but at the same time, I can see why it would have alienated so many who had been with the band since 'For Richard'. Yet this was the logical result of Hastings' developing songwriting and the refinement of those elements of the Caravan sound for which he was responsible. He had honed his skills until the meandering song structures and instrumentals had been tightened into a form that took those elements and made an adult pop: something that had the concise melody and some depth into which you could sink your musical teeth.

10cc were doing this. Pilot, Blue and Cockney Rebel had also mined a similar vein and had shown smart arrangements, clever lyrics, and concise melody could hit a commercial sweet spot. James Warren and Andy Davies were eighteen months away from the same things as their rambling Stackridge songs became more concise and then morphed into the short snappy singles of The Korgis. Of course, they had changed their identity to belay any confusion and prejudice. Would Caravan have to do the same thing? Could they actually do this?

Conclusion

As the events in the musical world of 1976 started to go against the bands of Caravan's generation and musical background, so their manager, who had promised so much, was running into a few problems of his own, which wouldn't help their case. There was also one more line-up change (no, really?) to take place before the next album.

Blind Dog took them another step forward. Unfortunately, the next album would be a step back from which, commercially, they were unable to recover.

Better By Far (Arista 1977)

Personnel:
Pye Hastings: guitar, vocal
Richard Coughlan: drums
Jan Schelhaas: keyboards, vocals
Dek Messecar: bass, vocals
Geoffrey Richardson: viola, guitar, flute, mandolin, sitar, vocals
Vicki Brown: vocals
Fiona Hibbert: harp
Tony Visconti: recorders, electric double bass
Producer: Tony Visconti
Recorded Utopia Studios London March-April 1977; released July 1977
No chart placing.

This should have been the step-up, the breakthrough into those commercial waters that Hastings' songwriting deserved at this point. That it was the beginning of a descent that saw Caravan break up and reform several times over the next five years, before an eight-year hiatus, is thus all the more disappointing. That it all went wrong was only partly down to the music. For this is not a great album, but its faults do not lay with the material, some of which is as fine an example of that intelligent pop song writing as you are likely to hear, and a couple of tunes that even hark back the progressive era, albeit in an economic format.

The first major issue for the band was, once again, money and management. Miles Copeland knew what he was doing and would go on to prove this in the 1980s and '90s with his management and record label successes. But back in 1976, following the release of *Blind Dog...*, and in early 1977 as the band prepared for the follow-up, BTM was in the process of going under. The culprit for this was Lou Reed. How did that happen?

During 1975 Copeland had been behind Star Trucking, a series of festivals across Europe that had been designed to promote BTM acts and to bolster their profile by bringing in some larger acts. Soft Machine were an obvious choice as they fitted in with the BTM roster and were at that point a large concert draw on the continent. The Mahavishnu Orchestra were a step up in fees and potential audience numbers. And then there was Lou Reed: still thought of in many ways as a cult figure in the UK, despite the patronage of Bowie, Reed was a guaranteed concert draw in mainland Europe and a coup for Copeland.

Or, at least, he would have been if he had bothered to show up for many of the shows. Admittedly, there had been death threats against him in Italy, and the Mafia had caused issues with protection for equipment hire (this was not unusual, as any reading of Henry Cow or Van Der Graaf's Italian adventures will show), but his no-show and the logistics of transporting the bill across Europe with the reduced ticket sales had crippled Copeland's business to the point where BTM went bust.

As a result, Caravan found themselves without a record label to operate between themselves and Arista, who simply did not understand a band who did not come to them gift-wrapped for the pop charts. They had a manager, but one who had worked out that there was a sea change coming in the music business, and it might just be that a band who were trying to evolve from their hippy progressive past into a clever pop group could not drag their old audience with them, and were tainted by their history for what was to come.

Punk was sweeping all before it that did not already have huge sales. Second division bands – of which Caravan were still decidedly one – were set to be wiped out by the tidal wave. Copeland and his brother Stewart knew this. The Police were the ex-drummer of Curved Air, a jazz bassist called Gordon who was a teacher, and in Andy Summers, a guitarist who had Canterbury roots with a brief Soft Machine stint and with Kevin Ayers, had just finished with Kevin Coyne and was old enough for Caravan members to have seen him with Zoot Money's Big Roll Band when they were still at school. A haircut, a bottle of bleach and some snappy tunes later, and Copeland's boys conquered the world. But not before Miles had embraced punk by starting Step Forward Records with Mark Perry of Alternative TV/'Sniffing Glue' infamy, as well as Illegal and Deptford Fun City, along the way issuing the first records by Squeeze and Sham 69. Later, he expanded this to IRS (a knowing nod to the US tax agency, to whom he probably paid rather a lot of cash), which had huge hits and took the new wave into the American mainstream.

None of which was any help to a band who were looking to become the next 10cc in terms of how they could be perceived. Punk didn't harm Rod Stewart, Fleetwood Mac, Electric Light Orchestra, or even 10cc themselves, all of whom already had a huge sales base and coverage. But it did kill off Burlesque, Deaf School, and strangle City Boy's progress so that they faded rapidly. All three dealt with sharp, clever rock that had pop hooks. All three were industry tips for greatness. None of them carried the now-to-be-perceived stigma of their past.

Why am I telling you all this? What does it have to do with Caravan? Well, in these days of heritage bands, the internet, and the space that this makes for all kinds of music to find an audience of some kind, it's easy to forget how hard it was to be noticed and make an impression back then. One national radio station. One national 'serious' rock show and one chart show. A few regional programmes and a smattering of local radio – commercial radio was only a few years old in the UK at that point. Four weekly music papers and no monthly glossies. The TV and radio were geared to sales and what the pluggers had to offer. The weekly press carried ads for anyone who would pay, but their writers were geared to what was on ground level. And that wasn't anyone like Caravan (or a hundred others who would have got column inches a year or so prior): to be a band like that, you had to have record company clout and strong management to survive. Caravan had neither.

Then you have to factor in that the current zeitgeist was about being street level, about not showing ostentatious wealth, about getting back to basics. This was partly because of the mores of punk rock but also because the country was going through a period that had seen the three day week about to bleed into the winter of discontent. They were grim times, and I am well aware that I am sounding like social historian Dominic Sandbrook, but this does have significance, as the sleeve of the new album was almost guaranteed to make the band look out of place, ridiculous, and the last thing you'd want to be seen under your arm as you walked out of a shop in 1977.

The front of the sleeve is set in a banqueting hall, with four of the band gathered around a long table, dressed in bow ties and tuxedos, having enjoyed a lavish meal and getting stuck into the brandy and cigars. At the back, by the fireplace (with obligatory roaring fire), stands the fifth member. There is a glamourous lady in flowing dress dancing attendance, a young lady in the distance, and an obsequious butler. On the reverse, the band are gone and the butler and the two ladies relax.

You can only wonder what they were thinking when they agreed to this photo shoot: what kind of image does that put across of the band at any time, let alone during that era. It's a truly terrible representation of a clever, musical and witty band. And here's another thing – you have Hastings, Coughlan, Richardson and Schelhaas around the table, while it appears that new bassist Dek Messecar is consigned to the background, although having the compensation of a very attractive young lady to talk to, unless he hadn't been recruited at that point, and so a stand-in was sent to the back of the (very large) room. I do remember being very embarrassed by this sleeve when I first bought the album, and I still consider it a huge error of judgement. The sleeves of their next two albums may have been basic and dull, but at least they created no impression, rather than one that was so negative.

But what of that new bassist? Dek Messecar had previously played in Darryl Way's Wolf and so had the Curved Air/Copeland connection. Wolf were very much a 'serious' progressive band, with complex arrangements and themes that straddled classical and jazz voicings as much as rock. They made three albums for Decca and had sold relatively little despite some decent notices. When the offer to reform the much more bankable Curved Air came up, Way knew which side his bread was buttered, and so Messecar, drummer Ian Mosley and guitarist John Etheridge found themselves jobless. Messecar had not contributed to the writing but had proved himself a dextrous and melodic bassist who had sung lead on the first album but had a voice better suited to back-up. Mike Wedgewood had quit because of better offers – an arranger and bassist of his skills and commercial range was always in demand. Geoff Richardson had also been doing more sessions, as had Schelhaas. Hastings and Coughlan were the band, not hired hands, and had publishing to sustain them. Make no mistake; this album was supposed to crack the big time because it had to.

Hence the hiring of Tony Visconti, who had real commercial clout and was a man with an ear for how to make a band radio and mass market-friendly. With no Jimmy Hastings, this time, and just Fiona Hibbert's harp and Visconti himself adding recorders and stand up bass to one track, this recording at Utopia was supposed to polish the band's new songs for radio.

So how did he make such a cock-up of it? To my ears, because he simply smoothed out too many of the edges in the actual sound so that instead of being radio-friendly, it just became anodyne and far too smooth. There's not a lot of bottom end, but that wouldn't matter too much if not for the fact that the guitars are denuded of any bite at all, and the keyboard sounds are at times almost fairground-like – perfect for cheesy chart pop at that time, but too far removed from the core sound of the band to fit. And perhaps, as a result, some of the performances are so restrained as to sound almost flat; lacking in energy. When they aren't, then this is still a good album, and it's frustrating to hear it straining at the edges of how good it could have been.

'Feelin' Alright' (Hastings)
Not that you'd know it from opener 'Feelin' Alright', which is not the Traffic song but a Hastings tune that is about the joys of pulling. He did love a George Formby-styled lyric, and the band kick in energetically from the opening drum flurry and beat, although it has to be said that the keys sound is terrible. It's very catchy, upbeat, and a good opener.

'Behind You' (Hastings)
'Behind You' follows, and is a splendid tale of the perils of messing about with someone else's wife, even if he is massive and is out to do you some damage. This is 'Keeping Back My Love' with new lyrics and has an added funky solo section from Schelhaas and some nice guitar lines added. The problem here is that the guitars are quite weedy compared to the original version – just a little more crunch, and this would have been splendid. The lyric is probably one of my favourite Hastings end-of-the-pier stories. It also gives us a first chance to hear Messecar as he underpins the song and proves he is from the light-fingered Perry school of playing. It stands in contrast to the third song on the vinyl side one.

'Better By Far' (Hastings)
'Better By Far', the title track, is a lovely ballad melodically in which Mr Hastings explains that it is far to better to have loved and lost than never have tried at all – even in the back of a bus or the seat of a car. It has a sweet guitar solo and some nice harmonies and is the first track to be completely suited to the production. It could have been a big radio track – the only issue perhaps being that back then, the irresistible urge Hastings had to shoehorn the odd double entendre and naughty joke into even the most heartfelt of lyrics may have put off some radio producers (but then 10cc – them again – could get away with things, so why not?).

'Silver Strings' (Richardson)

'Silver Strings' is a Geoff Richardson tune and the first of two in a row from him. It's a strong commercial pop song with hints of soul and disco in the arrangement and a light viola solo that shows a sense of musical playfulness, ending on a catchy synth hook. It's witty, but the kind of song the more 'prog' Caravan fans feel is all wrong and too pop, showing they have perhaps misunderstood what the band is about in some ways.

'The Last Unicorn' (Richardson)

Whereas Richardson's 'The Last Unicorn' is a six-minute summation of what prog rock was: starting with a viola theme, this instrumental moves through a shuffling march beat that has keys supporting the theme before mandolins lead to the recorders wistfully fading ... only for the bass to drive a theme over which the guitars and keys soar in unison before Schelhaas cuts loose over a propulsive rhythm, weaving melody into which a guitar cuts a swathe of notes, taking over the lead. It builds to a breakdown that takes us back to the main theme via a mournful flute melody. It's a sad and haunting piece, harks back to other times, and shows they could still cut it when they wanted - and that's the key word.

'Give Me More' (Hastings)

Side two begins with 'Give Me More', another of Hastings' funny lyrics about an odd woman he falls for. It's a got a touch of the Max Millers about some of the lyrics and shows just how out of step perhaps Hastings was at this point. The melody and arrangement are again very radio-friendly, and as this is not guitar-led, then the lack of bite does not matter. As the song progresses, the lyrics get more and more like a British sex comedy: this was a time when the British film industry was sustained by Robin Askwith and leering window cleaners, and it does seem that Pye was hankering after a job writing songs for these films!

'Man In A Car' (Schelhaas)

'Man In A Car', Schelhaas' sole songwriting credit for the band, is up next, and the less leering lyric is actually a bit of a relief. The song is built around some almost blues-rock voicings on the verses before changing tempo for the chorus, which leads into a synth line hook that would sound better if the keyboard sound wasn't so cheesy. A brief flute and cymbal-led breakdown releases the tension and sets up a reprise for the second half of the song. To me, the synth hook is good, but what it needed was a vocal hook to match, which it doesn't quite have. It does have more of that lovely flute-and-keys wash breakdown to come, though, so I can live with that.

'Let It Shine' (Hastings)

'Let It Shine' is Hastings getting his mind out of the gutter and all the better for it. A guitar flurry leads into a catchy opening riff and then a song that is all about positivity and is incredibly upbeat, with some lovely arrangements on the verses that carry the vocal along. It's a great pop song and has some real singalong potential to it. Again, just a bit more crunch on the guitars and this could have been single material. Of course, whether it would have got radio play is debateable at this time, but by the time you reach the anthemic solo, you think a decent plugger could have got them a summer hit from this.

'Nightmare' (Hastings)

From this latter lyrically positive note, the album ends atmospherically with 'Nightmare', which is the kind of longer song they were writing a few years before (was it really only four years since *For Girls*...? Things moved fast back then for a working band). Sweeping guitar and cymbals presage a Hastings lyric that is heartfelt and some splendid viola lines before the next section, which needs a harder edge to the sound for the change in mood to really work. The melody carries this through, though, to a reflective guitar solo from Richardson that roams over a backdrop that evokes an incoming tide, building to a repeating and overlapping guitar figure that emphasises the wave motif.

Conclusion

And there we have it. A fade out in more ways than one as Caravan were floundering on those very rocks their last track here evoked.

The Album (Kingdom 1980)

Personnel:
Pye Hastings: guitar, vocal
Richard Coughlan: drums
Geoffrey Richardson: guitar, viola, flute, vocal
David Sinclair: organ, piano, synthesiser
Dek Messecar: bass, vocal
Producer: Terry King/Caravan
Recorded Farmyard Studios Little Chalfont, Bucks July 1980; released October 1980
No chart placing.

Better By Far was not a bad album, but it was compromised by its production, its cover, and its timing. That was one hell of a combination and saw the band start to flounder. Geoff Richardson parted company with the band as he was too busy with sessions to commit himself. It was amicable and understandable. The same could also be said for Dek Messecar, who had walked in at the wrong time. There were abortive sessions to record another album for a blatantly disinterested Arista, with a returning Richard Sinclair, fresh from Camel, coming back in on bass and vocals. However, things fell apart when Arista dropped the band. No deal, no management – it looked like the end was nigh. This last line-up dissolved, and while Schelhaas went back to sessions, Coughlan hung up his sticks and began a career in pub management.

This left Pye Hastings alone but determined to carry on, recording with new musicians in an attempt to land a solo deal. They say that timing is everything, and when you are trying to go solo with a past that isn't big enough to ensure audiences, but big enough to maybe hamper you in the then-current climate, then that is more than ever true, and no amount of good songs will change that. The recordings for both the aborted Caravan record and the solo album lay in the box for sixteen years until Pye's son, now old enough to join the family business, dusted them off and got them a release. But more of that later.

Back at the end of the seventies, Hastings hung up his guitar and started a career in heavy plant management (construction, not forestry). However, King was still around in the business, and he had a plan. Get the boys back together with a 'star' line-up, do some touring, and record a live album. The Marquee was already planning its 25th anniversary year, and there were a number of venerable '60s and '70s rockers limbering up for that.

Hastings and Coughlan persuaded Geoff Richardson to come back, and the Sinclair cousins were also on board. Attempts to record some live shows didn't quite work, and Richard packed his bass and left once more, giving reason to call up Dek Messecar, who joined up for the ride. When the accountants figured out that it would cost no more to record a live album than a studio one, Hastings, Sinclair and Richardson got their heads together and came up with an album's worth of material, including a song from Jim Atkinson, a friend of Richardson's (which incidentally makes him the only non-band member to contribute other than Mike Ratledge – unless you count John Murphy's co-writes).

The Album was an unimaginative title, and it was housed in an equally unimaginative sleeve of black with the band name and title in big yellow/gold letters. It was probably done in a hurry; as was the album, seeing as it was recorded in July 1980 and released in the October of that year. It shows, really. Again, the songs are let down mainly by the production, which is no-frills and quite toppy. It misses a good bottom end to ground it and the guitars a bit jangly and shrill for my liking. It also suffers from keyboard sounds that are of their time and don't really suit the band (though I will admit that this latter could partly be down to my own expectations of how they should sound). The studio was The Farmyard in Little Chalfont, Bucks. Not exactly Air or using the Manor Mobile, and it shows. It was produced by the band and Terry King himself, which I suspect was more about him keeping an eye on that budget than anything creative.

The record was released to universal apathy in the UK, where the band were at this point considered dead and buried. France was a slightly different matter. The first track on the album, 'Heartbreaker', was released as a single and even got them a spot on French TV, which you can find on YouTube. Being Caravan, of course, even this backfired – their spot was cut short for the news bulletin announcing the attempted assassination of the Pope. It seemed like nothing could go right for them.

Even so, there was enough interest stirred by this in France for Terry King (who noticeably had either been unable to secure a deal for the band or else had decided to keep complete control this time around) to get a license for and release the Fairfield Halls concert from 1974 in that country. As 'Caravan's Greatest Hits', obviously…

But what of the record itself? It follows on from *Better By Far* in being comprised of shorter, more pop-oriented pieces. This is not surprising: Sinclair had been moving this way in their writing during David's last tenure in the band, five years before; for Hastings, this was just the natural progression in his own writing; and Richardson's own scattered pieces with the band had shown a flair for concise melody.

'Heartbreaker' (Hastings)
The album opener and single, 'Heartbreaker' is a pop-hook-laden Hastings song with a strong band arrangement and a concise guitar solo, thankfully free of any nudge and a wink lyrics. I say thankfully as this could have garnered some serious Radio 2 airplay at the time. You may say that isn't what Caravan should be about or aiming for, but the fact is that this is glossy, catchy pop that would have given them the material success they deserved.

'Corner Of Me Eye' (Richardson)
'Corner Of Me Eye' is a Richardson song that follows his 'Silver Strings' contribution to the last album, in that it mixes a number of different pop

genres into the arrangement and has a wit about the way it switches from a soul riff to a guitar section that is almost a hoedown in style, before breaking into an instrumental break that could be FM-friendly rock. The nostalgic lyric is about nicking your mate's girlfriend when at school, and the opening and closing chords have 'hit' written all over them.

'Whatcha Gonna Tell Me' (Sinclair)

'Whatcha Gonna Tell Me' is a solo Sinclair write, and oddly starts with a Jethro Tull lite guitar/flute riff, and is littered with those kind of guitar fills along with an electric piano solo. It's a strange song for 1980, as it harks back to a progressive style that was not Caravan's. Even stranger when you consider how much more commercial Sinclair's co-writes with Murphy were at this time. There is a nice flute/piano breakdown in the middle, and as ever, it's littered with melodies and hooks in the instrumental sections. The odd thing is that the bass seems so toppy here that it could almost be a rhythm guitar – that's one of the things that has always bugged me about this record. Was it just using a cheap studio at a rushed pace? If so, it's a pity.

'Piano Player' (Sinclair/Murphy)

Speaking of those Sinclair/Murphy co-writes, next up we have 'Piano Player', which is a tune about what it's like to be the player in the corner, observer but never participant. Sung by Hastings, the song has a good chord sequence and a tasteful arrangement. It's a good song, but as will also be apparent on the next album, although Sinclair and Murphy were writing songs that could have garnered any number of covers from established pop and middle of the road artists, it doesn't sit well with Caravan. Until that is, we reach the bridge, and an instrumental section led by the viola brings us right back on the Caravan tracks (see what I did there?) and all of a sudden, it becomes a Caravan tune into the middle eight, which is vaguely reminiscent of the Beatles before it goes back into the lounge pop of the first part of the track. With that in the middle, it just about works. I'd love to hear someone else do it, although the fact that it ends with the piano player dying might put a bit of a crimp in that. It does give us a nice instrumental fade, though.

'Make Yourself At Home' (Sinclair)

Another Dave Sinclair solo write ends the side with 'Make Yourself At Home', which is ... baffling. Again, it's not a bad song, but it sounds like something he may have had knocking around for a few years as it would have been a good mid-'70's single for a pop act. It's catchy, has a good breakdown in the middle with some random voices, and just before that, a brief but heroic guitar solo. Whereas the rest of the side can be fitted into the time period, if not actually being typical Caravan, this is oddly out of place.

Above: The original line-up, Richard Coughlan between moustaches, and obviously the gig rider did not include chairs!

Below: The current line-up in France in 2016. Jim Leverton wonders if Jan Schelhaas has popped off for a quick glass of vino.

Left: The first album cover. Verve placing them on a pedestal prematurely (as it transpired). (*Decca / Verve*)

Right: A more characteristic shot for the second album. You wouldn't think it was the middle of West London, would you? (*Decca*)

Left: *In The Land Of Grey And Pink.* The defining album, by far: but did that sleeve pigeonhole them unfairly in the eyes of some listeners? (*Decca*)

Right: A touch of the Hogarth's: for *Waterloo Lily* if you look at the inner sleeve and the contrasting images, then it becomes a perfect visual description of the contents. (*Deram*)

Left: *For Girls Who Grow Plump In The Night*. A slightly risqué title and a soft-focus romantic image. This album sums up the musical and lyrical tone of this period. (*Deram*)

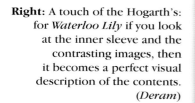

Right: The use of an orchestra was an interesting experiment as an album, but what does this cover actually say? Perhaps that confusion sums up the end of this era for the band. (*Deram*)

Left: 'A Place Of My Own' on *Beat Club* in 1969. Mr Hastings throws a chord shape…

Right: … while Sinclair D. ignores such showmanship and plays immaculately (as usual).

Left: The whole band on *Beat Club*, except that Sinclair R. finds himself expunged by a dodgy camera effect.

Right: 'Golf Girl', *Beat Club* 1971, and Sinclair R. now knows how to dodge the camera effects while Mr Coughlan hits that hi-hat.

Left: Meanwhile, a mirrored Sinclair D. continues to eschew showmanship for dexterous one-handed playing.

Right: Another chord shape from Mr Hastings, strictly rhythm with no crying or singing at this point.

Left: The promo film for 'The Dog, The Dog…' – Messrs Perry, Coughlan and Richardson find themselves mesmerised by another display of one-handed dexterity by Sinclair D. (the Davoli synth solo).

Right: Mr Coughlan wondering if it was time to grow back that 'tache…

Left: …while Mr Richardson wonders if he should tell him that it definitely is while he plays yet another splendid viola phrase.

Right: The 'Heartbreaker' promo from 1980: Mr Hastings looks like a pop star while Mr Richardson wonders if it's too little too late…

Left: In order to counteract this, Mr Richardson plays like he's in The Jags or The Vapours. If they'd changed the band name, it might have worked (it did for Stackridge, after all).

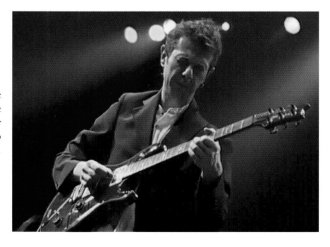

Right: Doug Boyle in the early 2000's. He's a fine player whose relatively few studio contributions echo his live skills.

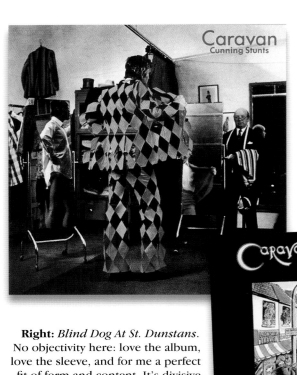

Left: A lovely Hipgnosis sleeve from the last Decca album, *Cunning Stunts*. An album with the same musical sleight of hand, going from intelligent pop to concept pieces with consummate ease. (*Deram*)

Right: *Blind Dog At St. Dunstans*. No objectivity here: love the album, love the sleeve, and for me a perfect fit of form and content. It's divisive for the more prog-tastic fan, though. (*BTM/Arista*)

Left: And then there's this: *Better By Far*. Seriously – what were they thinking? So out of step as a sleeve, but musically, a decent album neutered by Visconti's touch. (*Arista*)

Right: The Kingdom years. This is not the sleeve I had for *The Album* – this is from the later reissue – but just as cheap and unimaginative, and does not serve the record well. (*Kingdom*)

Left: *Back To Front*. The original line-up is ill-served by this, as well and I'm sure my mum had a print from Marks & Spencer's by the same artist. (*Kingdom*)

Right: *Cool Water*. The 'lost' recordings, given a suitably atmospheric sleeve. It's very apt, too, as Messrs Hastings and Coughlan were the great survivors. (*Pony Canyon*)

Left: *Bedrock,* filmed in 1990: The band were slightly ring-rusty, but it got things going again.

Right: Pause to salute Jimmy Hastings, a man whose talent runs through the band's music and still the man behind the best sax solo on a progressive rock album ever (see *In The Land Of Grey And Pink*).

Left: Mr Coughlan, having decided in 1973 that yes, he will go for that 'tache again, shows how he has become a master of that particular art.

Right: Mr Hastings croons – he didn't sound warmed up at the time, but that didn't last long.

Left: Sinclair D. uses both hands here – it is the 90's, after all, as that shirt (on loan from The Happy Mondays) proves.

Right: Sinclair R. played and sang superbly on *Bedrock*, but I can't get past that hat.

Above: Playing The Summer's End Festival in Lydney, 2011. Messrs Leverton and Hastings in full flow. (*Photo: Tim Ellis*)

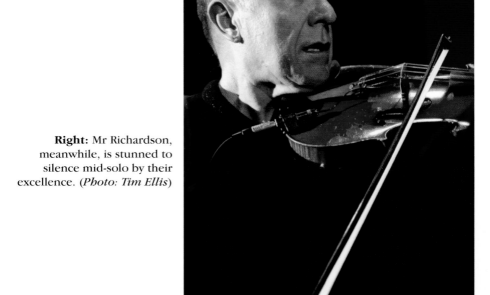

Right: Mr Richardson, meanwhile, is stunned to silence mid-solo by their excellence. (*Photo: Tim Ellis*)

Above: Mr Hastings on top form. Beyond warmed up (as he wasn't during the *Bedrock* performance), he was on fire by this time. (*Photo: Tim Ellis*)

Below: Jan Schelhaas finally appears in a shot! About time, as his work in the band has been invaluable and superb. (*Photo: Tim Ellis*)

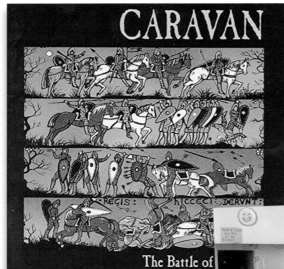

Left: *Battle Of Hastings*. Now this is the halfway decent cover for this album from a later reissue. There have been some that may put you off buying it completely. (*Castle*)

Right: *The Unauthorised Breakfast Item*. There's something fishy about this cover (and you know Messrs Hastings and Coughlan would have made the same joke). (*Eclectic*)

Left: *Paradise Filter*. The most recent album of new songs (at time of writing). An elegiac, melodic and mature album, yet still with the old quirks and eccentricities that fans grew to love. (*Caravan Records*)

Right: *The Back Catalogue Songs*. And possibly the last album? Who knows? If so, to hear this line-up run through their take on classic Caravan recorded cleanly in a studio, is a fine way to mark their part in the long history of the band. (*Caravan Records*)

The Back Catalogue Songs

Left: Universal/Decca compilation that is probably the best starting point for those looking to track back. Nice sleeve, too. (*Decca*)

Right: On the other hand, how not to do a sleeve: one era represented on the cover, when it's another Decca-spanning compilation, and with some cheap graphics. (*Decca*)

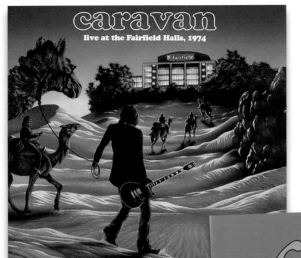

Left: A splendid live album, released in part on compilations, and once as a 'greatest hits' (I know). Does Mike Wedgewood still get sweaty palms thinking of this night, I wonder? (*Decca*)

Right: *A Hunting We Shall Go: Live in 1974*. Quite a nice sleeve for a bafflingly poor release. (*The Store For Music*)

Left: *The Show Of Our Lives*. The best catch-all BBC sessions album. Not quite complete, but certainly the easiest way to pick up the majority of sessions.

'Golden Mile' (Atkinson)

And so we start side two of the old vinyl with Jim Atkinson's guest write for the band, 'Golden Mile', which is apparently about a Spanish holiday. Or artists (of some sort). It does have a great scratchy rhythm guitar and funk bass. And lyrics in French, so don't ask me. But what it does have in abundance are instrumental and vocal hooks and an infectious feel. It's another track that may seem to be 'not Caravan' at first glance, but in fact it mirrors some of the styles outside rock they had been toying with since *Cunning Stunts* and Mike Wedgewood. No solos in this, which is unusual, but you don't notice it until the song is over as there's so much going on instrumentally.

'Bright Shiny Day' (Hastings)

'Bright Shiny Day' follows; another Hastings song that is a companion piece to 'Let It Shine' on the previous album. It's a love song about being back home with the one that you love and starts with some guitar hooks that lead into the vocal. In this sense, it's a formula song, as many of those written by Hastings over the last three albums had this structure. But it's only the structure that stays the same. This has a melody that has a repetitive chorus line which leads into a section where Richardson delivers a melting flute solo before it's back to more vocal, couched in delicate keyboard fills around the gently strummed rhythm section. Don't be gloomy, don't be alone, be with the one you love seems to be the message. Old hippy or old romantic? It could be either, but mark my words, it was another radio ballad lost to its potential audience.

'Clear Blue Sky' (Richardson)

'Clear Blue Sky' is up next, wherein Geoff Richardson delivers a first: a Caravan reggae track. I can see the die-hard prog fans throwing up their hands in despair, and to be honest, that was exactly what the fifteen-year-old me did when I first bought the album. Why the hell did they want to sound like The Police? (Er, count how many records The Police sold?) And anyway, this was a little anaemic next to Bob Marley and Burning Spear. Well yes, it is, and the lack of bass end didn't help, to be frank. But – and there is a but – it was just an obvious exploration for Richardson after the soul and disco influences in his previous writes. And isn't 'progression' about trying new things? Anyway, the point here is that a bit of iffy scat singing is compensated for by a lovely keys solo, and even if the song as such is a bit of chorus and not a lot else, it does stretch out pleasantly over six minutes. Not a triumph, but a worthwhile experiment. Anyway, if 10cc could get away with 'Dreadlock Holiday', I suppose I can see where they may have been coming from.

'Keepin' Up De Fences' (Hastings)

And so to the last track. As the sudden last note of the previous track dies, the chugging rhythm guitar of 'Keepin' Up De Fences' lead into a Hastings tune that is a tour de force to end on, certainly by recent standards. It has the riffy intro, the verse that takes a sideways turn melodically before charging into a chorus section and some guitar soloing. This is the Caravan style distilled down to six minutes and given what was then, a modern sheen. The guitars are new wave sharp, the keyboard is a synth, not an organ, and the whole thing is just that tad faster and edgier. Of course, as this is Caravan we're talking about and not one of Miles Copeland's IRS signings; it's a little more old-school rock, especially on the second guitar solo, but as it fades out, you feel that maybe this album has aged better than most would imagine and that at the end of the day it's actually better than *Better By Far* in its energy levels.

CD Reissue extra tracks
'Heartbreaker' (single version) (Hastings)
'It's Never Too Late' (Hastings)
The CD reissue had the single cut of 'Heartbreaker', which as with some other single mixes in the catalogue, sounds exactly the same as the album track to me; and an extra Hastings song, 'It's Never Too Late', which is actually similar in feel to 'Bright Shiny Day', which may be why it was omitted. There can be no other reason (except perhaps time, as it would have unbalanced the sides and made cutting difficult, for this was still the era of vinyl), as it's of a comparable quality to his other writing in this period, and as with the whole album, the band sound tight and unified. That's the thing that comes out of this: it might have been a last gasp, and there might have actually been very few people out there at this point who wanted to hear them or could even remember who they were, but they didn't seem to give a monkeys. This album sounds like a band who are doing it for the fun of it and enjoying getting back in the studio, even in somewhat straitened circumstances.

It was like they knew it wouldn't last.

And it didn't.

Back To Front (Kingdom 1982)

Personnel:
Pye Hastings: guitar, vocal
Richard Sinclair: bass, guitar, vocal
David Sinclair: keyboards, vocal
Richard Coughlan: drums, spoken vocal
Mel Collins: saxophone
Producer: Caravan
Recorded Oak Studios Herne Bay, Kent, November 1981- Jan 1982; released July 1982
No chart placing.

With Dek Messecar, Jan Schelhaas and Geoff Richardson needing to earn a living and keep working in music, it was inevitable that the lack of success that *The Album* had would impact on Caravan. Pye and Richard could return to their day jobs and still be on call, while David Sinclair could return to the world of songwriting and publishing. For the other three, it meant that they had to, in effect, leave the band. Both Messecar and Schelhaas left music full-time: Messecar is a designer, and Schelhaas became a driving instructor, though his connection with the band turned out to be far from over. Geoff Richardson became a successful session player and arranger, a freelance lifestyle that enabled him to return once more when the call came and to become once again a mainstay for the band, missing in action only occasionally when dates clashed.

It looked like this was the end of that road, and the Caravan had been dragged down a dusty cul-de-sac, only to rust in a ditch. That's a terrible metaphor, isn't it, and also not a correct one, because – just when it seemed once more to be all over – Terry King had other ideas.

The upcoming Marquee anniversary that had prompted all of this in 1980 was still on the horizon, and as Richard Sinclair was currently at a loose end, might it not be a better idea if the original line-up got back together to play? And maybe tour and do an album? After all, King now had the record label, and he had that market in France where he knew he could turn a profit if recording costs were kept low.

So it was that the reunited band retired to Oak Studios in Herne Bay, Kent, and between November 1981 and January 1982 laid down what would become *Back To Front*. The title comes from a number of things. Firstly, there is the title track, the lyric of which discusses the back to front existence of being a musician and spending your life living in a different way to most of the population; then there is the fact that this is back to front in the sense of going backwards to the beginning in order to move forward; and again, it literally means going back to the front as the studio was near the promenade at Herne Bay, which is a minor Kentish seaside resort. Which, incidentally, has a very nice caravan park (my next-door neighbours at the time had a caravan in Herne Bay).

Of course, being financed by Terry King, the album is compromised by possibly the worst cover a Caravan album has ever had. A ghastly shade of mustard yellow, with a green and yellow etched design that resembles the kind of semi-abstract – flowers that turn into birds in flight with graded line shading – that was used for prints sold in the likes of Marks & Spencers at the time (my mum had some of these on the living room wall, and this sleeve reminded me of them), with lettering that looked like it came straight from a Letraset onto paper graphic, it did the band or the music no justice at all. This is possibly worse than the *Better By Far* sleeve, though not, obviously, as ostentatious (quite the reverse). It was an embarrassment to own up to owning, and was probably hidden at the back of many an album stack. It wasn't going to encourage the casual browser, that was for sure – though, by this time, it's debatable that a band like Caravan could have attracted many casual browsers.

Likewise, the sound was cheap. It was reasonably well recorded and mixed, but there was a poverty about the sound. The guitars were a bit scratchy where they needed to be fuller, and the keyboards sounded shiny and modern but cheap: like a Casio rather than a Yamaha. It stank of low budget, and the fact that it was anything other than pauperous in imagination was a miracle. Even given that the guitar sound may have been an attempt to stay contemporary (as with *The Album*), the music demanded a fuller, more rounded sound. Again, for me, there is not enough bottom end on the mix – but then, I do have a tendency to prefer more bass-heavy sounds, so that might be just personal prejudice.

I remember getting this new, being excited that it was a Caravan album when I thought they were gone for good; being even more excited that it was the return of Richard Sinclair (whose previous Caravan exploits and stint in Camel had made me a fan of his voice and bass skills); and then being a bit deflated by the sleeve.

The contents, however, do not ultimately disappoint, even though they are somewhat baffling; by turns exciting, thrilling, and then completely confusing. An album that perhaps defines the term 'curate's egg' more starkly than the last two albums, which, if you have been paying attention, you will have realised also fit that description. Because, as broad as you may be able to define it, there is a certain Caravan style and sound, and even when they stepped outside it on *Better By Far* and *The Album*, they still managed to retain a certain something of themselves. On this album, they return to familiar tropes more fully than on those albums and also manage to step completely outside anything that can be said to fit them in any way.

This is down to David Sinclair, whose three writing credits on the album achieve the astounding trick of being the two songs that sound completely out of place, and also then one song that takes them right back to the way they sounded stylistically a decade before. That's quite some achievement. For 'Proper Job/Back To Front', the title track and album closer, we go back to something that could have come from the first two Decca albums in construction and melody, albeit tighter and less inclined to meander. Refined, and just what someone like me wanted to hear. On the other hand, what the hell was 'Sally Don't Change It' and 'Videos Of Hollywood' all about? They sound out of place, and at the time, I loathed them for this. As I've got older and haven't been bothered to skip them at the end of side one and start of side two (I still play the vinyl – never got the hens-teeth rare CD as there were no extras), I've come to appreciate them, even quite like them, and see them in a different light.

Context is everything: without it, understanding how and why anything happens is virtually impossible. These two songs ('Videos...' written with Murphy, 'Sally...' a solo effort) can be seen to fit into the idea of Caravan as a writer's band who are trying to reach a broader audience and transition to Radio 2 pop. Adult pop. Something that is hard to understand now in the world of heritage bands and seventy-year-old rockers. But back then it was only 25 years since Bill Haley and Elvis, and music was littered with bands whose time had seemingly passed and who were old hat, passed over and forgotten. The only way to sustain a career back then was to find a way to appeal to a wider, non-rock audience. Marshall stacks past forty were a no-no. It was a difficult time for sixties and early seventies bands trying to adjust, and it would be another decade before the concept of old bands carrying on just doing their thing would become commercially viable and another decade again before it became the industry that it has been since the millennium.

It may have seemed that for every album since 1975, we have been talking about a band that had made a series of missteps for every best foot forwards, but we mustn't think of them in being in isolation. Every band of their ilk was doing this, and many with far worse, less forward-thinking, and far more musically disastrous results than Caravan. For every Genesis, transitioning from progressive mavens to pop giants, there was a Gentle Giant, floundering in a sea of hard-rock-lite while trying to keep a sense of identity (I like Gentle Giant, to be clear, so no slight is intended). Caravan come somewhere in the middle of that, which is not bad artistically, even if it didn't help them commercially.

But what of the album itself, once you get past the bloody awful sleeve? Well, the first thing to say is that Sinclair R has returned, hooray! That unique songwriting style, that meanders and potters and talks about nothing in an amusing fashion while being hummable and quirky, and which had lit up early Caravan, and parts of the Hatfields and Camel, is back in full on side one, as two of the four tracks are down to him.

'Back To Herne Bay Front' (Sinclair)
'Back To Herne Bay Front' opens with a wash of guitar, ethereal keys, and seagull noises before going into the song, a relaxed shuffle, which is melodically meandering as Sinclair R goes into a description of the recording, the town and the pubs. Greasy fish and chips while not a lot of totty, by all accounts. It's observational, everyday, and has a chorus section that picks up

the tempo while not actually being a chorus as such (very Richard) before a lovely instrumental section that has keys and some lovely bass burbling before we're back to the song and we learn that the local Indian restaurant has closed down and it's not the Hotel California down here, you know. We even get some verité recording of the bingo on the prom. There's a nice keyboard hook in there, and the bass wanders delightfully all over the track as it fades out. The grey and pink lands in winter rain: it's not the same, but yet it is.

'Bet You Wanna Take It All / Hold On Hold On' (Hastings)

'Bet You Wanna Take It All / Hold On Hold On' is a Hastings tune that lyrically covers similar ground in that it seems to be about Hastings on the pull in a dank seaside town. Pity they didn't record in Hastings as I could do a Hastings in Hastings gag. Just as well, then. There's something about Pye's lyrics that makes me want to do this. Anyway, the song itself is riffy and hooky in the first section, with some piano from Sinclair that almost makes me think of Chas 'n' Dave, which is not as bad as it sounds, as it has that seaside feel to it that fits the theme so far. The second part of the song sounds like it's actually a completely different song shoehorned in, slower and ruined by a sax solo from guest Mel Collins, who then honks over the reprise of the first section. It's a personal thing, but I've always thought Mel Collins was over-rated. The man can play, of course, but I've always felt he lacks subtlety, and that shows here.

'AA Man' (Sinclair)

No matter, he's mixed down in this section, and before you know it, we're back to Sinclair R and 'AA Man', which starts with a sprightly guitar riff from the man himself, who also plays a guitar solo. It's another observational lyric about having a car that's packing up and getting stranded on the hard shoulder when the engine goes west. It has an actual hook and chorus, and some melodic verses into which he scans lines that shouldn't really fit. It's a unique talent he has, and here the arrangement is ably supported by some crisp drumming, electric piano in the verses, and some guitars that are jangling and suit the song perfectly. The guitar solo is interesting in that it sounds to me like the kind of lines he'd play on bass, just transposed to a six-string.

And now the first of the two problematic tracks.

'Videos Of Hollywood' (Sinclair/Murphy)

'Videos Of Hollywood' is beautifully sung by Sinclair R, with a great catchy tune and wistful feel that suits the nostalgic lyric about the golden years of Hollywood. The arrangement is tasteful and dynamic, and the sax solo even fits, as its brassy tone is suited. There is also a great synth line preceding it. The problem here is that it would be great covered by someone like Barbara Dickson or Elaine Page, using this backing track, and is a fine piece of work in its own right (down to the lovely bass solo, which is brief, plays the melody and is sublime): but it bears no relation to anything else Caravan had ever recorded. Even when they were trying more commercial styles, they still sounded like Caravan playing another style. Here they sound like a different band and it's just out of kilter.

'Sally Don't Change It' (Sinclair)
It's not much better when you flip the vinyl and get to 'Sally Don't Change It', which is actually a lovely and heartfelt ballad which Sinclair D wrote about his wife at the time and is prime singer/songwriter material. Its weakness is that Dave is no lead vocalist – apparently Hastings felt uncomfortable singing it as it was so personal, though he was originally slated to sing. At 16/17, I thought it was sappy and out of place. I still feel the latter, but now I'm decades older, I know what he's talking about, and it's lovely to me. But again, it just doesn't fit.

'All Aboard' (Hastings)
'All Aboard' is next up, and another of Hastings' songs about positivity and feeling good. It has a strong melody and is spoiled only by the synth sound on the solo, which just doesn't suit the song. It's the straightest pop song in the Caravan style on here and sets up nicely for…

'Taken My Breath Away' (Hastings)
Now then, this is an odd one lyrically, with Pye going back to his British sex comedy lyrics diverting to B-movie horror. I'd love to know what he was watching during the seventies. It's another foray into reggae, only this time there it's the full 'Dreadlock Holiday', with an actual song. There's some marvellous supple bass playing on this, as it slips from reggae rhythms into something a little more pop by the time we get to the last choruses, which are Hastings at his hooky best.

'Proper Job / Back To Front' (Sinclair)
And so, we come to 'Proper Job/ Back To Front', wherein Sinclair D delivers a song about being a musician and songwriter, getting grief from everyone, and with Richard Coughlan doing a spoken word section that must have made him think of what his dad told him. The lyrics are about making it, and does anyone understand? It has a great opening riff that is reprised, and a section with a sax solo that may make me rethink what I said about Mel Collins, as he delivers a fine performance (still not Jimmy Hastings, though) before the band move into a heavier riff section that has a squalling guitar solo and ascending chords to a piece of keys heroism. All the elements of those older, long Caravan pieces are in here, condensed and spoilt only a tad by those bloody keyboard sounds. Then it's back to the main riff and a reprise of the song where all the money disappears, but the music remains (was Terry King listening?) before finally going into an ascending riff section that builds instrumental tension and layers of arpeggio over the top from guitar and synth for a full two minutes before sweeping keys cut it dead, with only an echo remaining.

Conclusion

This is the oddest album in the catalogue to approach because of those two songs that sound so out of place, and yet the rest of it is the best 'Caravan' album for some time. If you can appreciate the two odd songs for what they are, then it's actually a record that deserves serious reappraisal

Cool Water (Pony Canyon 1994)

Personnel:
Pye Hastings: guitar, vocal
Richard Coughlan: drums (tracks 1-7)
Richard Sinclair: bass (tracks 1-7)
Jan Schelhaas: keyboards (tracks 1-7)
Rod Edwards: keyboards (tracks 8-11)
John Gustafson: bass (tracks 8-11)
Ian Mosley: drums (tracks 8-11)
Jimmy Hastings: saxophone (tracks 8-11)
Producer: Julian Gordon-Hastings
Recorded 1977-78; released October 1994
No chart placing.

I'm dealing with this one here because of the chronology of release, so it was the first time that Caravan fans got to hear the material, but it dates back to the period post-*Better By Far* when Geoff Richardson and Dek Messecar had left, and Richard Sinclair had rejoined. I'm a bit torn about this, really, as if Caravan had finished the album and had got a release for it with a subsequent tour, then the good Mr Sinclair would have been committed to this and would not have ended up joining Camel and contributing to *Rain Dances*, which is another of my all-time favourite records (which is selfish, I'll admit).

So, what we have here are the seven tracks that had been recorded for a new Caravan album before Arista pulled the plug and Miles Copeland's money-antennae had directed him towards punk. On top of the uncompleted album, we have four tracks recorded with a different set of musicians that were intended as part of a Pye Hastings solo album.

As pontificated on earlier, there was no real demand for this by 1977, and to be frank there never really had been: back in the day, after *Waterloo Lily*, the material written for *For Girls* had been intended for a Hastings solo record, and it was only pressure from management, bookers and record company that persuaded him to keep the Caravan name. He was not alone with this problem: at the turn of the 1980s, Robert Fripp was persuaded to change the name of Discipline to King Crimson as it was the only way to get bookings and a deal. Similarly, Black Sabbath's *Seventh Star* was intended to be a Tony Iommi solo album until the record company revealed they would not release it unless he used the Black Sabbath name for guaranteed marquee value. At least no-one went as far with Caravan as Cliff Davies did with Fleetwood Mac when he managed them, and sending out a group of unrelated musicians under that name to fulfil bookings (they changed their name to Stretch and wrote their hit single 'Why Did You Do It?' about him).

As primary songwriter in the mid-to-late seventies, and again when the band reconvened (as we will see in a few pages), Hastings must have found it frustrating: Caravan was a band, but who was writing and singing the majority of the music? Yet the attitude was one of 'who is this bloke'? It would take until 2017, and a Caravan hiatus brought about by other members commitments, for Hastings to finally issue an album under his own name.

Meantime, a casual peruser of these pages may be wondering how on earth a bunch of unreleased recordings from the late seventies got released almost two decades later by a band that seemingly no longer existed? Twenty five-plus years on, this kind of thing is common for the rock collectors market, but it wasn't the norm back then.

Of course, the key here is that the band did still exist, albeit in a slightly altered form from what you got on this release. So how did it get from the petering out of the *Back To Front* era to here?

The key to this lay with the *Bedrock* TV series. Put together by ATV, as explained later, this series revived and reunited a number of cult '70s bands from the progressive era, putting them into the ATV studio to record live sets that showcased the material for which they were best known. In the case of Caravan, it meant that after eight years, the four-piece who had recorded the first and last Caravan albums were reunited. Things went well, a live video and CD eventually emerging of the programme (as it did for most of the featured acts), and deciding to stay together on an ad-hoc basis, they began to tour sporadically. But it wasn't long before Sinclair R did his usual disappearing act to form his own Caravan Of Dreams (with Camel compatriot Andy Ward), and as Geoff Richardson was only too happy to come on board again, having a good relationship with Messrs Hastings and Coughlan of many years standing, he was perfectly placed to recommend a bass player with whom he had worked, and who had a lengthy rock'n'roll history. This is where Jim Leverton – of whom more later – enters the story and stays: the longest-serving bass player in the history of the band.

Meanwhile, this sporadic activity and the interest it had stirred caused Pye's son Julian, who was a recording engineer and moving into production, to persuade his father to let go of the tapes, which he had retained from Arista, and let Hastings Jnr mix them and look for a deal, which he found initially with the Japanese Pony Canyon label (a home for bands who had history but were forgotten in the homeland – the NWOBHM band Preying Mantis have had a career in Japan for decades when they are nothing but a memory in the UK, courtesy of a string of Pony Canyon releases).

And so, fans finally had a chance to hear these tapes. It's an interesting release, as the first seven tracks feature Hastings, Coughlan, Sinclair and Schelhaas and can be said to follow on from *Better By Far*; the last four are from the aborted solo sessions and feature different musicians entirely (although brother Jimmy puts in an appearance). Keyboard player Rod Edwards was an old hand – indeed, he'd been in Edwards Hand with Roger Hand, and before that, they had been Piccadilly Line. Mostly working as a duo, they had recorded three albums and also worked as producers and writers on Roger Glover's *Butterfly Ball*, as well as with Gordon Giltrap (where Edwards teamed up with

John G Perry). A tasteful pop-rock oriented keys man rather than a progressive keys wizard, this was surely indicative of Hastings' intended direction.

As a rhythm section, the solo tracks featured bassist John Gustafson, whose pedigree went back to Merseybeat and The Big Three, as well as Quatermass, Roxy Music, Hard Stuff, The Ian Gillan Band (in his jazz-rock period), and numerous sessions. The drummer was one Ian Mosley, last seen in company with Dek Messecar in Wolf (as an aside, Wolf guitarist John Etheridge, of Soft Machine and jazz renown, later depped live for Caravan in the 2010s), before drumming for Trace, Rik Van Der Linden's post-Ekseption ELP-lite trio. By the time these tapes emerged, he had been in the Marillion drum seat for a decade and so remained thereafter.

A different drummer: Hastings' writing was so closely tied to the way that Richard Coughlan played that this promised to be interesting.

'Cool Water' (Hastings)
'Cool Water' itself commences the album with a slow, supper-jazz opening and some ethereal piano scales before we slip into an equally slow ballad that had a hook line which reminds me of Peter Skellern. This is sophisticated adult pop-rock, albeit with the obligatory Hastings witty lyric about a little too much to drink. Restrained, smooth and with harmonies that drift over keyboard solo with a chord change in the middle that just throws you enough to make sure that you're paying attention, and with a nice bass line at the conclusion.

'Just The Way You Are' (Hastings)
'Just The Way You Are' is a straight love song, uptempo and brisk. It has the kind of straight rock changes that hark back to the kind of thing they might have played in The Wilde Flowers, albeit with a veneer of sophistication; and some lovely supple bass underneath the piano and guitar, with Coughlan laying a backbeat like he hadn't since the first Verve album. They may have been paying attention to the fact that others were getting back to basics, but this is a very Caravan way of doing it.

'Tuesday Is Rock And Roll Nite' (Hastings)
'Tuesday Is Rock And Roll Nite' is the kind of song that would make a Caravan purist shake their head, and at fourteen, I would have joined them. It starts with a riff that could have come off a Savoy Brown album and rolls along like 10cc playing Status Quo, with a playful lyric. This either shows a splendid sense of humour or a growing sense of desperation and the search for the zeitgeist. Given the two tracks before, I'd opt for the former, especially as Schelhaas throws in a nice synth solo. What's wrong with rocking out? Nothing – although three tracks in from that sweet jazz ballad intro, it does smack of looking for a direction. It makes you wonder how much pressure they were under at this point: personally, I think Hastings, who is the only songwriter at work here, is responding with verve.

'The Crack Of The Willow' (Hastings)
'The Crack Of The Willow' is – surprise – about cricket, amongst other things, and begins mid-tempo with a synth melody that catches the ear and leads into a Hastings lyric and an arrangement that smacks of a summer afternoon in Kent on the village green. The synth melody line, which is laid-back and wistful, comes back in again. Sonically, this fits in what would have been the previous album, but even unfinished and mixed at a later date, it has more life in it than Visconti had managed. Listening to this, one does wonder how much that misjudgement affected the band: given how lovely but out of step with the world of 1977 this is, that's possibly irrelevant.

'Ansaphone' (Hastings)
'Ansaphone' follows, with a creeping funked-up riff and some nice synth horns punctuating a slow guitar riff underpinned by some great bass – and then it right-turns into a typical Hastings melodic chord construction and chorus that sounds at odds and yet is as glorious as it is unexpected. The lyric is another lad-at-the-mercy-of-womankind Hastings special, and there is a solo from Schelhaas in which he gets his keyboard to imitate a sax to good effect, with some great piano runs as we plunge into the second half of the song. This sounds like it would have fitted the *Blind Dog* period very nicely.

'Cold Fright' (Hastings)
'Cold Fright' continues the funkier theme – does a funky Caravan really work? – as the riff on bass leads the song, with Coughlan busy on the hi-hat to good effect as Hastings deals out one of his patented insult lyrics as he laments a man who just wants to be a in rock'n'roll band but is slapped down at every turn. Heartfelt, considering their position at that time? Possibly, but this musical turn puts them firmly in that adult territory that was later exploited by Sad Café. There's a strong, twisting guitar riff that comes in just over halfway through, allowing Schelhaas to pound the piano to good effect. Oddly, this lacks a strong vocal hook, which is usually one of Hastings' strengths.

'Side By Side' (Hastings)
'Side By Side' brings the actual Caravan recordings to an end with a mid-tempo song that has a lilting opening guitar riff before leading into a song of love lost. It has the feel of an album closer, the big song at the end of side two, with a chorus that utilises the guitar refrain as a melody and, in an alternate world, is a bit of a 'wave your lighter in the air' moment.

Overall, the Caravan material comes to about 35 minutes, a short album and maybe one song short of being complete. It would have been a better album than *Better By Far* as there is a greater continuity of sound, but there are moments when it sounds like a band that are just out of time and trying to work out what exactly people – business and audience – want from them.

Now to the solo sessions.

'You Won't Get Me Up In One Of Those' (Hastings)

'You Won't Get Me Up In One Of Those' is a song from a confirmed fear-of-flying advocate with an amusing lyric. It sounds like Hastings and yet not: Mosley and Gustafson kick up a jerky, almost calypso-like version of funk, yet it's stiff as a board. Mosley is undoubtedly a good drummer (listen to those Wolf albums from a few years before), but this has no swing and misses the easy propulsion of Coughlan behind the beat. It has radio and novelty potential as a single, mind you.

'To The Land Of My Fathers' (Hastings)

'To The Land Of My Fathers' is on more familiar territory from the off, as it kicks off with some gorgeous Jimmy Hastings sax before leading into a ballad in which Pye waxes lyrical about Scotland, with brother Jim playing under the vocal line. It has some good playing by Gustafson that atones for the odd style of the previous track and has a vocal refrain that seems to go on forever before a great descending chord sequence closes it. It has anthemic potential and is a splendid example of where he may have gone.

'Poor Molly' (Hastings)

This is unlike 'Poor Molly', which is a chugging rock'n'roll tune with an irritating bass line that punctuates the sound and gets in the way of the melody. This could be 'Tuesday Is Rock And Roll Nite' as written for Status Quo ... and then halfway through, it hits a typical melodic Hastings twist that lifts it up for the second half. It's not bad – but that's the problem: it needed to be more than that at the time.

'Send Reinforcements' (Hastings)

On the other hand, 'Send Reinforcements' is a big Hastings ballad with a dramatic arrangement around it, played with restraint and poise. It has a big chorus and is one of his 'feelgood' songs, a particularly rich vein he was mining at this point. I find it deeply ironic that he was writing the kind of songs that old rock bands were having US hits with a decade later and was roundly ignored and written off for it: wrong place, wrong time.

Conclusion

So, what does this amount to? Well, if *Better By Far* hadn't stiffed, then the Caravan tracks here could have made more inroads in the States if Arista had retained interest and got behind them. The backwards step of that last album knocked that one on the head, and in the UK, they were dead in the water, which is a shame as it's a decent record, if a song light. The solo recordings are 50/50 between a direction and a search for one and right then, it needed to be more than that.

Finally, nice to note that the recording for some of this was by Maurice Haylett, who had stayed on board all the way through and should really be thought of as a non-playing Caravan traveller.

It was nice to see this out there, but it didn't really represent where the band was at in its reconstituted form. For that, we had to wait another year.

The Battle Of Hastings (Castle 1995)

Personnel:
Pye Hastings: guitar, vocal
Richard Coughlan: drums
David Sinclair: keyboards, vocal
Geoffrey Richardson: viola, violin, clarinet, guitar, mandolin, percussion, vocals
Jim Leverton: bass, vocals
Jimmy Hastings: sax, flute, clarinet
Producer: Julian Gordon-Hastings
Recorded Astra Studios Monks Horton, Kent, April-May 1995; released September 1995
No chart placing.

The early to mid-nineties were an odd time musically. It was still pre-internet, but those people who had been fans of sixties and seventies bands and had dropped off their interest when kids and life and work had got in the way of such fripperies as music. Well, they now had time to look back and wonder what happened to their favourites. There was a thriving sixties oldies circuit, and more bands from the seventies were starting to reform in the belief that there was an audience for them. The beginnings of the heritage rock gig and festival circuit that we know nowadays was starting to blossom. The kinds of seventies bands that were reforming at this point tended to be mainly those who had a cult following or had been flops at the time but whose reputations had grown in the interim; mainly bands whose music could be said to fall into the psychedelic or progressive milieu.

There were reasons for this: since the mid-eighties and the first psychedelic revival, followed by the neo-prog wave that followed on from the new wave of British heavy metal, it could be argued that most guitar-based rock bands were no longer moving forward: it was as though a plateau had been reached in terms of how far the form could be taken, and so many fans of the form had started to look back at what had come before. Certainly, it's not hard to argue that Britpop, which was in full swing when Caravan made this album, was backwards-looking in form and that any progression or ideas of forward momentum were to be seen mainly in dance, rave and electronica as they developed, rather than guitar-based rock. This looking back had also provided a boost to the record collecting fraternity, who it must be said were primarily male, of a certain age, and made the market the most lucrative for dealers and bootleggers in rare progressive and psychedelic records. This spurred some small labels into specialising in reissues, sometimes with extra tracks added as a purchasing incentive. It was a small market but a loyal one with purchasing power. Labels like See For Miles, Demon, Charly, and Bam Caruso were mining this vein profitably, soon joined by Beat Goes On.

In the middle of this, Castle Communications started to expand their operations: beginning by putting together cheap double-album compilations of larger cult acts and some who had experienced a degree of fame first time around, they expanded into more niche marketing by starting Sequel Records, which delved into the archives of bankrupt label catalogues they had purchased. They also noted the limited success European labels like Repertoire and SPM had achieved by putting out new releases by reformed bands.

There was a market, albeit a small one, but profitable if mined correctly. There were also bands who were drawing decent audiences based on past exploits and the fact that the new line-ups could deliver. One of those, of course, being Caravan.

At this point, Caravan were in a position that made the past struggles with record companies seem to be moot: the band were no longer a full-time occupation, but a paying hobby for Hastings and Coughlan, and a part of their income for freelancers Richardson, Sinclair, and new boy Leverton. If a label approached them to record an album, then it was simply a matter of getting paid for the recording, agreeing the deal, and making sure that there was some promotion to ensure people knew it was available. Indeed, under the new conditions of the market, it was even possible to record yourself and license the album out, ensuring that you regained control after a certain period. There was less risk for the label and less pressure on the band: no-one expected to make a chart album anymore, to gain hit singles (unless by fluke), and there was no longer big money at stake. The odds on each side were evened out.

I have explained this in great detail as, a quarter of a century later, it's important to look at the context in which the next batch of albums were recorded and released, as the conditions and expectations of both record company and band had an influence on the content, just as they had in the seventies and early eighties. It's also a very different context to the way albums are made and disseminated by such 'heritage' bands in the 21st century, as market conditions changed. The music is all that matters, but it's not the only thing: a paradox, but an unavoidable one.

Yes, the music: many bands were plying their back catalogue alone and had nothing new to offer. That wasn't true of Caravan: Pye Hastings does love a tune, and he does love to write. That much is obvious from the fact that having reintroduced the band to the new CD market by gaining a release for the *Cool Water* material, he now had enough new songs for the band to go into the studio with Hastings Jnr in the production seat and lay down the eleven tracks – all of which were Hastings songs – that constituted *The Battle Of Hastings*.

Now there's an album title to conjure with, as it not only harks back to a historic Kentish event in British history, but it also could denote the battle in the studio between father and son over the recording and the material, with the additional input from Uncle Jim, as Jimmy Hastings also contributes to the album. It's also possible that it's a hint of a battle for control over where the band was going, as it's notable that there are no David Sinclair songs on this album, even though he was an established member of this line-up. I think we can all predict where that one is going, but in the meantime, we have an album that is cursed once more with a terrible sleeve on some issues – the one with the cartoon Bayeux tapestry sleeve is nice, though. Pay no heed, as although the contents are not the absolute return to form that some may have wished, they do show a band that was still willing to adapt to the styles of new members and to try and do something a bit different within the parameters of their established style. And 'style' is the word, as Hastings has his trademarks and quirks both melodically and lyrically that make his songs recognisable and consistent across the entire catalogue.

At this point, we had Hastings accompanied by trusted lieutenant and pub landlord Richard Coughlan, who is as consistent and reliable as ever. Somewhere back at the start of this book I mentioned that he is probably under-rated as a drummer and he is never showy, at the service of the music, and just does his thing with consummate skill. The same is true here and continues on until his poor health curtailed his tenure. Meanwhile, alongside these stalwarts, we have Sinclair D, who has been behind the keys since the 1990 reformation, and Geoffrey Richardson ('It's got strings? You can blow down it? Give it here, I'll get a tune out of it.'), ensuring a strong instrumental front line. Now is the time to introduce Jim Leverton, the new bassist: he's still in situ, so deserves a proper introduction.

Jim Leverton is from Kent, as is the core of the band, but his musical journey was a little different. He had just joined when this album was recorded and was recommended by Richardson, who had worked with him from the early nineties when they had gigged together and formed a partnership that has seen them record duo albums together. At that time, Leverton was playing with Rory Gallagher and had just come out of a stint with the reformed Blodwyn Pig. A delve back into his history reveals a harder, blues-rock edge to his background than you might expect from a Caravan recruit.

He had started his recording career with Noel Redding in The Burnettes and The Loving Kind before Redding was recruited by Jimi Hendrix. Leverton then played sessions for Tom Jones, Gilbert O'Sullivan and Engelbert Humperdinck before Redding called him up to join his post-Experience band Fat Mattress. A couple of albums later, the band split and Leverton joined Juicy Lucy and then Ellis, the hard rock band put together by former Love Affair vocalist Steve Ellis. He followed this with a spell in Hemlock, the band formed by Miller Anderson from Keef Hartley's band (and with whom he recorded on Deram, coincidentally) before he followed Anderson to Savoy Brown for the *Boogie Brothers* album and tour, which saw Anderson and Stan Webb join Kim Simmonds.

Having survived that experience, Leverton played with Joe Brown and was then introduced to Steve Marriott, with whom he played in various combinations until Marriott's untimely death in 1991.

Seemingly more suited to a harder style than you would expect for Caravan, Leverton is actually a very adept and agile player whose strength is actually in rooting the music. Not a fussy player, as a rule, he slotted in beside Coughlan and gave the music breathing space that it sometimes had not been allowed by previous bassists. He also took over the Sinclair R vocal part on 'Nine Feet Underground'. Perhaps it says most about him that it's now hard to imagine another bassist in the band.

'It's A Sad, Sad, Affair' (Hastings)

The album begins with 'It's A Sad, Sad Affair', which continues the concise song style of latter-day Caravan. Bright chords and a melancholy lyric, with some nice mandolin embellishment and a swelling organ on the chorus, this is not perhaps what you'd expect if you hadn't caught the band since the *Bedrock* reunion (that'll be me, then), but it's a great, bright opener.

'Somewhere In Your Heart' (Hastings)

The following 'Somewhere In Your Heart' has a multi-layered arrangement with the viola and keys laying down a backdrop for another mid-tempo song about love and loss, which has a chord sequence on the chorus that draws you in, and a guitar solo that aches.

Two songs in, and the casual listener would be thinking it's all gone a bit Dire Straits and MOR. That's true: but these are middle-aged men writing and playing music that has more experience to it than twenty years before. It reflects what they and the audience have been through, and – most importantly of all – it does this and still retains that characteristic sound and quirk: the flute at the end of '...Heart' is a grown-up 'Golf Girl'. Listen to them back to back.

'Cold As Ice' (Hastings)

'Cold As Ice' starts with ethereal sounds and an almost whispered vocal before the band come in with a chord change in the chorus that seems to skip and catch you out, making you pay attention to the melody. Particularly of note here is the viola playing to counterpoint and accompany the vocal. Another romantic lyric – three songs in and no smut? – with an end that sees drifting flute, which is dream-like.

'Liar' (Hastings)

'Liar' is a faster tune with a strong hook line and a lyric about a cheating heart. The lyrics are far more mainstream and less full of idiosyncrasy than before. Did they have one eye on Radio 2, still, after all these years? Why not: these songs are strong enough, and the organ swelling under here also gives it a throwback feel, especially with the squealing guitar solo under the repeated hookline.

'Don't Want Love' (Hastings/Hastings)

'Don't Want Love' is a mid-paced ballad which is introduced by some splendid piano from Dave Sinclair, who so far has not had the chance to step forward. When we get into the song itself, the construction is very much around the vocal, with instrumental flourishes building only on the chorus and into the middle eight, where the piano once again gets foregrounded, with some melodic flourishes in there that are typically Sinclair. The second half of the song breaks it down for a flute solo to come in. Jimmy Hastings plays beautifully on this album (but then doesn't he always?).

'Travelling Ways' (Sinclair)
'Travelling Ways' again starts with piano leading into an uptempo tune that is sung by Richardson, and it suits his voice (good call by Hastings). A song about the joys of hitting the road, it has a great ascending chord sequence in the middle with mandolin and flute before we come back to the chorus and a flute that sounds more like piccolo or pipes to finish.

'This Time' (Hastings)
'This Time' has a lead guitar hook to pull us into the song, which motors along at just above mid-pace, the continuing lead hook punctuating the verses wherein Hastings gives us a song about love the second time around. As always, the arrangement serves the song, and there are some nice keyboard touches around the lead guitar. By this point, the first time listener may be reflecting that we've had little of the tempo changes and complex arrangements of the earlier versions of the band, but somehow this doesn't matter when Dave Sinclair unleashes a splendid solo. The point is that, although Caravan was still playing older songs in concert, this selection reflected where they stood at this point.

'If It Wasn't For Your Ego' (Hastings)
They still had the quirkier and more humorous side, as evinced first by 'If It Wasn't For Your Ego', which starts with choppy, fast chording that harks back to the late sixties, and a Hastings lyric about a friend whose infuriating and unwarranted self-confidence makes them intolerable. It slows for the middle eight sections before changing back to the choppy chords and a synth line from Sinclair that is sublime.

'It's Not Real' (Hastings)
'It's Not Real' starts with an anthemic chord sequence that leads into another straight romantic lyric and an arrangement that harks back to the first couple of tunes on the album, with the same swelling organ flourishes punctuating the vocals. If I had one complaint about the album, it would be that the arrangements, in being so focused on the song, sometimes tend to repeat. However, crashing guitar chords and a nagging riff that come in half way through change this and set up an organ solo with sweeps and vamps that take us back to the days when you could see Sinclair listened to Brian Auger. The organ carries into the next verse, and the energy level ramps up, with that nagging riff now driving on for some embellishment from Jimmy Hastings' sax, which powers the song to its finish.

'Wendy Wants Another 6" Mole' (Hastings)
Country picking, clarinet, and a nudge-nudge lyric? It has to be 'Wendy Wants Another Six Inch Mole', as Hastings laments being a civil engineer but has his life redeemed by Wendy's demands. Eccentricity and smut, it had to break out at one point, even with some decidedly strange sound effects. Short, and not what you would call sweet, but undeniably Caravan.

'I Know Why You're Laughing' (Hastings)
Which just gives us the album closer, 'I Know Why You're Laughing', which starts with some lovely Spanish guitar playing over a slow first verse, before it picks up into a mid-paced rocker that is the closest they come to Dire Straits territory. Now, I've never really liked Dire Straits, but when Caravan do this style, they make it their own, as the crashing chorus line shows: it's the Hastings songwriting style, making anything his own by the melodic signature. It's another serious love lyric, too: it could have been a hit. How many times have I said that? Especially when the anthemic guitar chords break out for some FM rock and a soaring synth solo in the last minute and a half.

Conclusion
This is a mature Caravan album: adult pop rock. It represents where Hastings was headed nearly twenty years before until stymied by circumstance.

Of course, being Caravan it somehow figures that what they did next was a little eccentric.

All Over You (HTD 1996)

Personnel:
Pye Hastings: guitar, vocal
Richard Coughlan: drums
David Sinclair: keyboards, vocal
Geoffrey Richardson: viola, flute, guitar, instrumentation
Jimmy Hastings: sax, flute, clarinet
Producer: Julian Gordon-Hastings
Recorded 1995-6; released 1996
No chart placing.

So, what do you do when you have a band on the road, reconnecting with audiences that remember you fondly, and you have a new album with new material in the can that reflects where you're at now? How, one wonders, do you consolidate that?

Well, if you're Caravan, what you do is make a bunch of home studio recordings wherein you reinterpret some vintage material in a new and interesting way. Even better, you make two such albums, one which looks at the very beginnings of your career and another which reinterprets a period that isn't remembered so fondly by admirers but is of importance to you as an artist.

It is, perhaps, a reflection of the era in terms of how vintage bands were seen by their public and by record companies that Caravan could do this, when a couple of decades earlier, both public and industry would have seen it as baffling and career suicide. So how did this come to pass?

HTD were a label based in Kent. They were artist-focused and also willing to take a chance on anyone they had loved. Founded and run by Malcolm Holmes and the late Barry Riddington, they weren't averse to new music (as they showed when HTD morphed into Talking Elephant); they just had a fondness for the bands and artists they had loved when they were younger. Which happened to include anyone who had been in Fairport Convention, as well as Uriah Heep, Amazing Blondel, Renaissance, and anything associated with Tony McPhee (they lost money on Egypt, a band of one-time 'Hogs, and were saved when Tony McPhee allowed them to put out a live album they had only recorded for their own fun, the profit saving them). They had put out two albums by Richard Sinclair's Caravan Of Dreams, so signing the actual parent band was a no-brainer. Holmes and Riddington were motivated by their love of the music and so put out some albums that seemed to be completely averse to sales and were strictly for fans only. (In this sense, they are similar to the still extant Angel Air and have that label's similarly annoying penchant for licensing at will and thus giving people like myself a headache when we try to sort out discographies. It all pays them, though, so fair enough).

HTD were the kind of label who liked an eccentricity, and also understood in a way that labels run by businessmen first and fans second could never comprehend, that the hardcore Caravan fan may be grown up enough to love the new material, but also may miss some of the inherent English daftness and sense of humour that ran through their veins.

What better way, then, to demonstrate this by giving Caravan a two-album deal that would enable them to revisit some old material that may not necessarily have been part of their current set and to look at it with fresh eyes.

This is an interesting selection of material, spanning the very first MGM/Verve album up to *For Girls...* with the inclusion of the almost obligatory 'Memory Lain, Hugh / Headloss.' As Geoff Richardson has often remarked on the riff being one of the first things Pye Hastings showed him, it seemed fitting that he would at least be playing on something here that he had played on the first time around. At the other end of the scale, we have 'A Place Of My Own', which came from the very first album. The bulk of the material otherwise was from *If I Could Do It All Over Again* and *Grey And Pink*, with only one piece extracted from *Waterloo Lily*, which is perhaps indicative of the dual nature of that album. Of course, it has the ubiquitous 'For Richard', but surprisingly only one section of 'Nine Feet Underground' in 'Disassociation'. 'Hello, Hello' and 'If I Could Do It All Over Again, I'd Do It All Over You' are fairly obvious choices as they are Hastings-penned and sung (as well as supplying this and the subsequent release with their titles), but to pick 'Golf Girl' and 'In The Land Of Grey And Pink' with Richard Sinclair nowhere to be seen can be viewed as brave or simply an attempt to mark them as Caravan songs that could still be performed by any line-up.

Speaking of which, this home-brewed concoction was performed without Jim Leverton, who at the time recording commenced had not joined (though he does appear on the companion album, up next). Instead, there is no credited bassist and the bass lines are either played on other instruments, uncredited or simply not present, which allows for a freedom in the instrumentation that a full band approach would not give. Produced once more by Julian Gordon-Hastings and with Uncle Jim providing the sax, clarinet and flute as ever, Pye Hastings and the ever-present Richard Coughlan were joined by Geoff Richardson on viola, flute and instrumentation ('that watering can will work with a bit of hose on it...') and David Sinclair on keyboards and vocals.

What we have here is an album that is much more freewheeling in nature than anything that Caravan had produced for more than two decades, with a sense of playfulness and fun that lends itself well to the cottage industry nature of the recording.

And before we plunge in, it's worth noting that 'Asfoteri' is retitled as 'Asforteri25', as it should have been twenty-five years before, and for that 25% that had caused so many problems (and was still to do so in the future, as King's continued ownership of *The Album* and *Back To Front* have made it difficult to get those albums reissued over the years, the Eclectic reissues being hard-fought to get licensed and slipping out of print quickly).

So, without further ado (suggesting some ado had taken place – an old joke that Pye Hastings probably wanted to work into a lyric over the years), let's press on.

'If I Could Do It All Over Again, I'd Do It All Over You'
(Hastings/Sinclair/Sinclair/Coughlan)
We begin with 'If I Could Do It Again, I'd Do It All Over You,' in which the
rhythm is substantially altered by the addition of a strummed acoustic guitar
that turns this into a shuffle over which the vocals are subordinate to some
splendid electric guitar, viola and sax breaks before we get an acoustic break
and some a cappella vocal leading into a complete sung verse. It has a laid-
back, jazzy feel that conjures up sunny afternoons in a completely different way
to the original.

'Place Of My Own' (Hastings/Sinclair/Sinclair/Coughlan)
'Place Of My Own' now becomes an acoustic guitar-led ballad that has a flute
and percussion break that is quite gorgeous, before the song comes back in
with some soaring vocal harmonies, and it becomes a song about searching for
inner peace.

'The Love In Your Eye / To Catch Me A Brother' (Hastings/Sinclair/Sinclair/Coughlan)
'The Love In Your Eye / To Catch Me A Brother' sounds almost identical vocally,
but the new acoustic treatment gives it a more laid-back feel. The theme
instrumentally running through the first half of this album is that of being
unplugged, and as you were unlikely to see Caravan on MTV, then this was as
close as you were likely to get. There's a nice bit of harmonica in this, a fine
Spanish acoustic guitar solo, and some lovely tasteful piano touches before the
second section kicks in with Coughlan upping the pace for Jimmy Hastings to
deliver a weaving and wandering flute line, the orchestral stabs replaced with
acoustic flourishes.

'In The Land Of Grey And Pink' (Hastings/Sinclair/Sinclair/Coughlan)
'In The Land Of Grey And Pink' has an extra acoustic riff added over the
initial chords that really catches the ear, and it's taken for the first verses as
completely acoustic and stripped back, with minimal percussion. A backwards
guitar solo sweeps in and is mixed in with a forward shadow of the same notes
to create a wonderful atmosphere. It's stripped back all the way through, in
fact, otherworldly, and Hastings sings it like Richard Sinclair was never there.

'Golf Girl' (Hastings/Sinclair/Sinclair/Coughlan)
'Golf Girl' is taken in the same manner, with the trombone riff replaced by the
same notes played in a different accent by a Wes Montgomery-styled electric
guitar. Taken as a slow, gently strummed song with viola drones on the
chorus, it has a very different atmosphere, breaking off to morse code and
wind effects, with odd sounds bleeding in and out in fine psychedelic style
before the strumming cuts back in for the trombone riff (now on flute) that is

double-tracked on the last phrase for a reprise of the strummed song section. The closing flute solo is now replaced by a reprise of the flute riff.

'Disassociation (Nine Feet Underground)' (Hastings/Sinclair/ Sinclair/Coughlan)
'Disassociation' starts with massed violas on the riff that precedes the song section, which, by rearranging the way in which the chords are strummed, Hastings makes his own. Violas and acoustic lead guitar bolster the arrangement as the song continues, gradually building around the repeat of the verses, fading it out with gentle acoustic washes where the harder guitar section enters in the original. It excerpts the song from the whole and makes it complete.

'Hello, Hello' (Hastings/Sinclair/Sinclair/Coughlan)
'Hello, Hello' now becomes a springing, propulsive riff that eschews the original jazzy swing of the original for a more consistent and head-nodding rhythm that draws you in, gradually realising that there is also delicate keyboard colouring behind the acoustic wash and percussion, with flutes added delicately to the mix before a sax solo sinuously weaves across the guitars, moving into the clockwork rhythm and three-chord end theme.

'Asforteri 25' (Hastings/Sinclair/Sinclair/Coughlan)
'Asforteri25' is a collage of rain, church bells, birdsong that gradually reveals the delicate filigree of the original acoustic guitar pattern, with percussion underneath, building up and coming out of the mist of the collage until the song itself is revealed, the simple chant of the lyrics – 'wish that I could be you', with flute climbing over the top to a fade – making you wonder if, given who the song was named for, there is some hidden sarcasm in the refrain.

'For Richard: Can't Be Long Now / Francoise/ For Richard / Warlock' (Hastings/Sinclair/Sinclair/Coughlan)
'For Richard: Can't Be Long Now/Francoise/For Richard/Warlock' is up next, with the strummed acoustic opening given some delicate piano accompaniment, the piano taking up the organ riff before distorted electric guitars take up the riff section playing off each other, their textures covering the bass frequencies as Coughlan keeps a straighter beat than on the original, for Sinclair to deliver the theme and variations thereof until the guitars crash chords and jam to the keyboard theme, returning and soloing over the top. Obviously, the opportunity to go a bit mental on this bit made them eschew the unplugged theme and then the guitars cut in and deliver the riff and the theme for the next section as though a grunge band decided to try and cover Caravan – no, really, and although that may sound oddly hideous, in fact, it works beautifully in this context.

'Memory Lain, Hugh / Headloss' (Hastings)

What someone who had only heard *The Battle Of Hastings* before would make of this is an amusing thought, as it crashes to the end and some dubbed applause which is carried over into 'Memory Lain, Hugh/Headloss' which is treated in the same electric manner, with some distant synth echoing the vocal line while the riff is played garage-band rough, with hard rock guitar notes echoing in the background. The crowd noise continues underneath while the 'band' riff their way through, the guitars glam-rock fuzzy with a synth solo spiralling over the top. This is not Caravan as you would expect to hear them, but it is a whole lot of fun to hear this piece simplified for rocking out, and you can see the smiles as they record it, the guitar grumbling on one chord for flute to come into the bridging section, drawn-out until it crashes into the final chords, with 'Headloss' coming on like Wishbone Ash playing Caravan with twin guitars on the intro and a straight-ahead rock rhythm. It's a simplified and stripped back version, shorn of all but the riff and vocal line and in so doing reminding us that Caravan never needed the frills and ornamentation to hide melodic deficiencies as some progressive bands did. The viola solo of the original becomes a squalling hard rock guitar solo and you find you're laughing at the audacity and also at how enjoyable it is in this form.

There are two extras that appear on some versions of this – as with all HTD releases, it can be a little confusing.

'Be Alright / Chance Of A Lifetime' (Hastings)

Anyway, a version of 'Be Alright/Chance Of A Lifetime' from *For Girls* returns to the unplugged ethos, with some emphatic guitar patterns and viola mirroring the vocal, until a single guitar line and vocal take over, joined by delicate Spanish acoustic lines. The use of this kind of acoustic melody throughout this album is perfectly placed, especially when flute is added to play alongside and then against the guitar melody. A massed bank of violas heralds the reprise of the vocal, fading out to distant acoustic guitars.

'If I Could Do It All Over Again, I'd Do It All Over You'
(Hastings/Sinclair/Sinclair/Coughlan) – single mix

The second extra is the single mix of 'If I Could Do It All Over Again...' and, aside from how barmy it would be for HTD to actually put this out as a single, there isn't much to differentiate it to these ears. Perhaps the electric guitar is mixed a little lower so that, especially on the opening verse, the vocal is more audible. The vocal section in the middle, with two Hastings vocals playing against each other, is more obvious, leading into the next full band verse. It ends with an unaccompanied reprise of the 'who do you think you are' vocal loop which has played virtually the whole way through, and which hits you starkly as a question that echoes in the silence that follows.

Well, that was probably how it was supposed to sound as the single mix, to be more impressive, but you just know that if it did get played, some clueless idiot presenter would talk across it inanely.

Conclusion

While this little hidden gem in the catalogue – worth it for the playfulness and the new slant on old favourites, sure, but more so for the sheer joy of how the new arrangements work – crept out, there was more to come, and this time with a full band in tow, including Jim Leverton and a surprising guest shot from an old Canterbury chum.

All Over You... Too (HTD 2000)

Personnel:
Pye Hastings: guitar, vocal, bass
David Sinclair: keyboards
Richard Coughlan: drums
Doug Boyle: lead guitar
Geoffrey Richardson: viola, violin
Jim Leverton: bass
Hugh Hopper: bass
Julian Gordon-Hastings: drum programming
Producer: Julian Gordon-Hastings
Recorded June 1999; released June 2000
No chart placing.

This second entry in revisiting the back catalogue is a little different, in that this time it features a full band, being a year later and with Leverton now bedded in. More importantly, it featured the very new boy Doug Boyle, who joined in 1996 and departed in 2007 – which means that although he did an awful lot of gigs, he only recorded this studio album and the next with Caravan, although he crops up on a number of live albums from this period (see later entries). Let's just stop for a moment and catch up on who this new recruit might be.

Doug Boyle is a bit younger than the rest of Caravan, having been born at the end of the fifties. This means he was old enough to have been a fan of them in their commercial prime (sounds odd in their case, but you know what I mean), but too young to have been playing in contemporary bands. His career as a working musician started a little later, and frankly, his first big gig was starting at the top, for from 1987 to 1992, he was in Robert Plant's band, which entailed recording and playing at the highest level. It's a mark of his skill that he hung around there for half a decade, and then from 1994, worked with Nigel Kennedy. It has to be said, Kennedy has a bit of a marmite public persona, but there is no denying that in his work, he has sought to break barriers between musical forms and bring together styles that may not have previously been melded. Like any seasoned experimenter, he's had things that have not worked, but the dedication is undeniable. So, for a guitar player to keep pace and contribute, it denotes skill and taste as well as undeniable chops.

Having Boyle in the line-up live meant that Richardson was not torn between viola or guitar on those tunes where he may have played both in the studio, and it also enabled Hastings to take another step back from soloing and stick to rhythm and vocals. As stated previously, Hastings is a good lead guitarist, but there seems to be something in his character that sees him prefer to let other players get that task and the limelight it brings. He is, undeniably, the leader – though whether he sees it this way is another matter – but in so being, does not see it necessary to impose that status upon his fellow band members.

For me, this is part of the character that has seen Caravan be such a good-humoured band over the decades and has made their music such a joy. Add the undoubted sense of humour both in the music and evident in performance, and you have a group who could never be accused of being 'serious artists' but who take the execution of their art seriously.

The only problem for me, personally, was that I always felt that in a live setting it was either a case of Boyle and Richardson getting in each other's way on older material or else leaving each other so much space that there were occasions when it seemed that one or other of them was just hanging around the stage waiting for their moment. This does not show on either this set of recordings, where Boyle is new and the excitement of a new guitar in town serves this set of revisits well; or on the following studio album, where he was in on the arranging process and so parts were worked out from the beginning.

Just to add to possible guitar overkill, Jim Leverton also plays guitar on the version of 'Ride' here, which the is the oldest track covered. Which conjures up strange visions of a front line of Hastings, Boyle, Leverton and Richardson all wielding the axe heavy metal style, with a baffled Coughlan and a reticent Sinclair being tempted out for a touch of the six-string. I have youthful memories of Blue Oyster Cult in their prime when all five members of the band would line up at the front of the stage with guitars as a part of the show. The idea of the terribly reserved and English Caravan indulging in such 'rawk' antics is quite funny (and perhaps would appeal to their sense of humour) or is that just me?

Moving swiftly on...

This set plunders a slightly later set of tunes from the Caravan catalogue than the previous album – it does have some very old tunes, but moves forward to the more pop-oriented years. The choice of 'A Very Smelly Grubby Little Oik' and a version of 'Bobbing Wide' with a later reprise are from *Blind Dog*, so obviously that pleased me; it's also nice to 'Stuck In A Hole' from *Cunning Stunts*, and an outing for 'Nightmare' from *Better By Far*, which was one of the best tracks from that album, and always unfairly neglected. 'Hoedown' and 'The Dog, The Dog, He's At It Again' are given a dust down from *For Girls*, and also from the latter we have 'C'thlu Thlu', which still stubbornly refuses to correct the non-Lovecraftian spelling.

An interesting selection – let's see what they did with it.

'Hoedown' (Hastings)

'Hoedown' starts with an orchestra tuning up over the beat before the guitars kick in and the song begins in earnest. There are some interesting, almost dub drop-outs on the first chorus, and for such a large line-up, this is about paring it down. The viola solo is followed by some more dub interludes as Julian Gordon Hastings brings a new ear to his father's work (it's amusing to think of them swapping ideas and arguments in the studio). This manages to keep the spirit of the original and also reinvent it completely at the same time.

'A Very Smelly Grubby Little Oik' (Hastings)
'Bobbing Wide' (Hastings)
A wonderful middle-eastern drum and viola part throw you off guard at the
beginning of 'A Very Smelly Grubby Little Oik', before the riff kicks in, and
the band attack it like a fuzzboxed version, with the lead growling while the
middle-eastern viola plays under at the end of each verse. Meanwhile, over the
top, Hastings sings it like it was 1976 still. It's a great tune and a splendidly
funny lyric. Then Boyle cuts loose with a concise solo that shoots us forward
twenty years before we get the last line, and segue into the first version of
'Bobbing Wide', with some nice organ stabs and more of that dub feel on the
rhythm, while the guitar cuts a jazzy and sharply melodic series of lines across
the top. Jim Leverton's bass is worth noting here as it underpins with a melodic
line that is sparse and unobtrusive but then catches the ear by dropping a beat
before coming back. Longer than the original and better realised.

'The Dog, The Dog, He's At It Again' (Hastings)
'The Dog, The Dog, He's At It Again,' starts with an electric guitar flourish
before an acoustic-led version of the song with delicate percussion that is
punctuated by electric guitar flourishes between the verses and some delicate
harmonies that support the lead vocal but don't attempt to build the wall of
sound that the original had, while viola weaves around them. When we come
to the riff section that was the bedrock for the original keyboard solo, this
time around, Boyle is given the opportunity to cut loose with a snaking solo
that uses a touch of wah-wah to wail over the vamp. Tension released, the
guitar winds back down the between-verses phrases and back into the song
for a vocal refrain, the electric adding chords to the acoustic base, with single-
note harmonies as the vocal round of the original returns before a fade on a
repetitive acoustic guitar phrase.

'Stuck In A Hole' (Hastings)
'Stuck In A Hole' begins with echoed, squealing electric over Coughlan's
drums and percussion before the song itself comes in, propelled along by the
insistent percussion. Boyle punctuates the verses with lines and fills, and it
seems obvious from here why they have recruited him. This is not the adult
pop band of a year before, good as they were, but rather a band that wants
to regain some fire. The twisting solo he delivers in the middle of the song
is confirmation of this idea. However, he does this without taking away from
the melody of the original song, rather, by playing around it. There is also a
knee-drop of the beat at the end of each riff that catches you off guard and
pulls you in, as well as some more dub ideas from our producer (I assume) to
give it an eerie edge: there is a track running underneath the song from the
second chorus on, mixed a little higher as we progress, that sounds like talk
radio recorded just off the wavelength (or distorted after recording), which is
disconcerting and divides the attention. It's a simple trick, but it really does

make you listen, when perhaps you might think 'oh yeah, but I bet it's not going to be like the original,' and your attention wanders.

'Ride' (Hastings/ Coughlan/ Sinclair/ Sinclair)

'Ride' takes us all the way back to the first Verve album, with Richardson's middle-eastern flavoured viola playing over the marching beat and some distant radio interference. It's 1969, you're on a break before your second album, and you've decided to check out Tangiers like William Burroughs. They've merged part of it for some reason, but if you put your ear to the ground, you can work it out. It straddles both and is perhaps a link missed by previous hearings. There's crashing guitar, a viola solo with some effects to distort the sound slightly, and some programmed drums between the percussion before it goes back to the raga-ish melody of the original, and more of that viola that takes you to a Moroccan market in 1969 – a mood then changed by a fluid, wailing guitar break from Boyle while the rhythm guitar riffs underneath. The solo continues on, taking you on a trip across the dunes, the hot sun playing down on you, as the sound buzzes in your ear and the beat of the camel's feet takes you closer to the fade-out – is that Radio Free Europe in the background, feedback, or a camel calling on the desert winds.

You get the idea. Glorious.

'Nightmare' (Hastings)

'Nightmare' is played relatively straight in the context of the rest of the album, with the guitars embellishing the first verse and Richardson's viola extemporisation double-tracked but still sticking closely to the template of the original – the backbeat on this version is more laid-back than on the *Better By Far* version, but this suits it as we go into the second vocal section, which has some tasteful guitar lines counterpointing the vocal lines before starting to flow and take over as the vocal ends and the chord sequence continues. Doug Boyle may be the new boy in town, but Hastings *pere et fils* are determined to give him his head and show what he can do – which he does beautifully on this section, supported by some excellent and unobtrusive piano accompaniment. This is one of the few times that we've really heard David Sinclair on this recording, and it's simple but effective as Boyle reproduces the end guitar lines of the original, like waves on a moonlit shore.

'C'thlu Thlu' (Hastings)

'C'thlu Thlu' starts with eerie and otherworld sound effects and distorted guitars on the riff that sounds like one is backwards. The distorted guitars continue through the vocal section, picking up the tempo until it reaches the slowed down, crawling riff once more. Sound effects and the vocal creep over the riff before it picks up the tempo once again. This is still very much a lesser Caravan song for me, and its inclusion here is baffling, but at least this version doesn't smack of Atomic Rooster. Of course, that kind of thinking is somewhat negated by what happens next, as suddenly it goes into the next riff section and Boyle cuts loose over the top with an atmospheric and effects-charged solo that makes you think this is not Caravan, surely? Who let the metal band into the studio on Caravan's coin? It's not really Caravan for me, but it is damned impressive and shows they were still keen on a bit of experimenting. The riff breaks down into stuttering chords with spiralling guitar over the top to the end and a cheesy horror-movie laugh. It does still make me wonder what Hastings was watching in the seventies.

'Bobbing Wide (Reprise)' (Hastings)

Still more surprises for 'Bobbing Wide' the reprise, which begins with an echoed drum machine and electronic pulses before guitar chords echo on the beat, with the organ faded in for rhythmic stabs and little fills, explosions in the distance, and that jazzy, sharp guitar line. The dub influence has been there all through this album, and here it really breaks out. Django Reinhart meets King Tubby in a thatched cottage, anyone? It could go on forever, letting you get carried along on its bouncing cloud (of what, I would not like to say), but before you know where you are, it's all over.

Conclusion

As with the previous album, given its nature, you wouldn't expect anything much from a set of virtually home recordings that were remakes – and yet in many ways, these are two of the strongest albums in their catalogue since *Blind Dog* and certainly their most progressive in the truest sense of the term since their Decca heyday. Musique concrete, dub, middle-eastern flavours, modern metal, all mixed in and added to the sounds we know so well? Don't tell me that's not progressive.

What the last three releases show is there have always been two distinct sides to the band, and specifically to Hastings and Coughlan, as they have been the only ever-present players. On the one hand, you have the dedication to the craft of songwriting and perfecting a kind of popular song that is witty, literate, melodic, and devoted to the art of being catchy without stripping back to a lowest common denominator: this is the side that gave us *The Battle Of Hastings*. And yet, on the other hand, you have the impulse that moved from the psych-pop of the initial album into the freewheeling desire to extemporise and play with sound – but never at the expense of melody – that ranged across the albums from *If I Could Do It All Over Again* through to *New Symphonia*. These two impulses, playing against each other, are never so starkly demonstrated as they are on these three albums, and it's ultimately what I believe most fans love about them.

Yet perhaps it's the very thing that prevented them becoming those stars of clever adult pop that they should have been?

The Unauthorised Breakfast Item (Eclectic 2003)

Personnel:
Pye Hastings: guitar, vocal
Richard Coughlan: drums
Geoffrey Richardson: viola, banjo, ukulele, acoustic guitar, vocals
Doug Boyle: lead guitar
Jim Leverton: bass, vocals
Jan Schelhaas: keyboards
Jimmy Hastings: sax, flute
David Sinclair: keyboards
Simon Bentall: percussion
Ralph Cross: percussion
Producer: Julian Gordon-Hastings
Recorded Astra Studios Monks Horton, Kent 2002; released 2003
No chart placing.

Well, it wouldn't be Caravan if everything went smoothly, would it? Even given that they were now definitely a part-time band with Hastings and Coughlan having careers outside the music business and the other players being session men and working with other groups, it's still a hell of time between the sudden burst of activity between the last three albums and this one. To be fair, it was worth the wait, as we will see, but what happened to stretch things out to nearly eight years?

Being Caravan, there was the inevitable line-up change, albeit one that would come as little surprise to long time band watchers. David Sinclair upped and left once again. This was put down to being about musical differences, and if the last remakes album was anything to go by, this isn't hard to imagine, as there's not much in the way of keyboards on it. But then, Sinclair D had always been an uneasy fit as a writer since the mid-seventies, despite being the man who penned 'Nine Feet Underground'. His songwriting with John Murphy had taken him in different directions, and in truth, he had a personal vision for what he wanted to do that didn't fit with the direction that Hastings and Coughlan were headed – the Captain and trusted lieutenant, with able seaman Richardson on board, if I can stretch that metaphor once more. It also didn't help that he was leaving the UK and moving to Japan: there are instances of bands who can continue to exist over the oceans, but they are few and far between, and with Caravan tours and festival appearances being in part dependant on pulling together already disparate calendars, then this would always be a bit of a stretch.

It was not an unfriendly parting of the ways, however, as Sinclair left them with a song that features on this album. And let's face it, given the nature of the Sinclair cousins, who would bet on them turning up for a Caravan 60th anniversary? And then leaving again, of course. Meantime, David Sinclair has found his metier by making solo albums on which he has guests and on which he can follow his own muse however he wants; and damn fine they have been, too.

Which left a bit of a gap behind the massed keyboards. Who else could Hastings turn to but old friend and ex-Caravan member Jan Schelhaas? Remember what Hastings said all those years back when Steve Miller joined: 'it's always easier to ask friends to join.' With Schelhaas, Hastings knew what he was getting, and there weren't going to be any musical shocks. The two men were living relatively close to each other, which made things easier, and for Schelhaas – who was still working as a driving instructor – the part-time nature of the band could be easily fitted around his more flexible day-job.

However, it was not this line-up changed that caused the delay. Neither was it lack of offers for work, as the heritage rock circuit was starting to take off, helped no end by the fact that the internet was starting to become the all-pervasive thing that it is today. Bands and musicians were starting their own websites to promote themselves, and there were a whole lot more online vendors, and these message board things that enabled fellow fans to come together and argue about whether or not Steve Miller should have joined (I still think his tenure was worthwhile) or which was the best organ solo David Sinclair ever played (too many candidates to list here) or just how big a moustache Richard Coughlan could grow (the answer being very large indeed). Of course, you wouldn't get that on a Megadeth forum, but you get the idea.

In terms of albums and recording, though, the internet was proving something of a conundrum: it threw up all these opportunities, sure, but it also had this thing called streaming and the mystery of mp3. The name Napster was being bandied around, and while the idea of file sharing to get some obscure bootleg from 1968 was good, and the idea that you could record any old thing and put it up there should anyone be fool enough to want it was also good (democracy of culture, etc.), it had some issues that had not been resolved: how did you stop someone sharing your new album and depriving you of sales that you may need not just to make a living but to actually repay any money you or a record company may have spent? These issues would dog the record companies who – like publishers with the idea of e-books – could not get their head around how to monetise a thing they couldn't hold in their hand. This would change the record industry. It would also open more doors for self-determination, as Caravan would find out a decade or so after this.

But in the late nineties and early noughties, the only safe bet for record companies and for heritage bands, were live albums, and so this is what happened with Caravan – most of the work Doug Boyle appears on is comprised of live recordings, which are all well and good but then tend to be safe (and cheaper to record, which is the additional reason record companies liked them), and have familiar songs in a new setting, but generally not so radically realised as Caravan had been doing.

Given the part-time nature of the band at this point, they needed a label that were prepared to put some effort in to make it worthwhile for their investment and who understood what they were doing. HTD had been a decent label and had worked with them on live releases as well, but they were fans first and businessmen second, and forever having problems. Castle were no more, having been swallowed up by Sanctuary management, the company run by Iron Maiden manager Rod Smallwood and funded by their success.

Enter Mark Powell: a former mastering engineer who had been working for some time as a consultant with larger companies and conglomerates on reissue repackages and retrospectives (his Decca/Deram label boxes, and the corresponding Vertigo box being of note), he now had a label called Eclectic which he ran with his wife Vicky, and which mixed reissues with some new releases. As a Caravan fan, he was the right man to make an offer, and so the recording and release of *The Unauthorised Breakfast Item* was ensured. Once again, Hastings Jnr sat in the production chair, and the band were augmented by Simon Bentall and Ralph Cross on percussion, as well as Jimmy Hastings on sax and flute, and a guest shot from David Sinclair on 'Nowhere To Hide', the song he bequeathed on parting.

There were additional percussionists on the album, as there were now live, as Richard Coughlan was starting to suffer from the health issues that would see him partially step down a year later after his diagnosis of rheumatoid arthritis. This would put a stop to live performances from 2005 until 2010, when the band recruited Mark Walker – although Richard would still play when possible, and continued to do so despite worsening health, until a stroke, and then his sad death from pneumonia in 2013 saw the end of an era for the band and fans.

As for Eclectic: the label had to fold in 2007 as cash-flow issues hit them hard when the record industry was failing to readjust to the digital age. Fortunately, his vision found a home with Cherry Red (whose accountancy-trained head Iain McNay has negotiated over forty years of balancing love of music and the books) and the Esoteric label he heads up for them has continued his mission.

That, however, was in the future. Back in 2003, we had a band headed back to the studio for the first time in over half a decade, with some serious road work behind them and a set of new songs – mostly by Hastings, but with that Sinclair parting gift and a first (and only) write from Boyle to add – to lay down.

'Smoking Gun (Right For Me)' (Hastings)
'Smoking Gun – Right For Me' opens the album with some very Dire Straits guitar and a tune and arrangement that puts us right in the same adult pop-rock territory as *The Battle Of Hastings*, with something of a first for Hastings – a lyric that has a message and meaning that is beyond his usual territory. He sounds like a man who has seen too much and is world-weary but never defeated. Guitar interplay lights up the mid-section, and the vocal melody is strong, moving into a middle-eight where the guitar plays round the vocal and Schelhaas brings in some subtle supporting synth chords. It's a great start and a statement of intent.

'Revenge' (Hastings)
'Revenge' starts with a dramatic chord sequence, a flurry of piano, and then into the body of the song, which puts Hastings the protagonist looking over his shoulder as he knows someone is out for exactly what the title says. There is some great piano in this, supporting and contrasting crunching guitar chords before the dramatic chords again and a melodic guitar solo. This is Caravan moving into AOR rock territory musically while still retaining the Hastings melodic style – there's even a brief punctuation of sax and a keyboard solo that apes the wah-organ sound of Sinclair while being very Schelhaas in style.

'The Unauthorised Breakfast Item' (Hastings)
A squelching wah guitar leads into the jaunty title track, which is very different in tone and is a metaphor – at least I think so – which centres around trying to pay for breakfast where someone has taken what they hadn't paid for, leaving Pye to carry the can. It's a witty and funny song, with the first fleeting appearance of the viola and the great 'tell me what the truth is / tell me where the fruit is' line just before a synth solo. After the sombre tone of the first two tracks, this is welcome light relief, and yet there's a hidden message in there (or am I just looking for it after those last two tunes?). On the face of it, though, a welcome Caravan touch of humour (with a great guitar line on the outro).

'Tell Me Why' (Hastings)
'Tell Me Why' is one of Pye's love songs, asking why she's leaving him. There's a great line about a stain on the wall triggering so many memories, and the melody has a great left turn into classic Caravan at the two-minute mark. Mid-paced and with a bouncing bass line to propel it, there is space for another guitar solo before a break in the rhythm arrangement emphasises the middle chorus. It motors along in the style that Caravan have revisited many times since the late seventies and has a gorgeous outbreak of fluting, fluttering keys that allow for a gently elegiac sax solo as the drums catch the beat and hold it in stasis.

'It's Getting A Whole Lot Better' (Hastings)
Delicate, faded-in chords herald 'It's Getting A Whole Lot Better', which is powered by a filigree guitar riff with some treated drums in the distance and discreet percussion so that Hastings can unleash one of his patented love songs with some delicate guitar playing around the viola and sustained keys in the background. Some simple, rooted bass playing from Leverton stops this floating away and keeps it grounded. Like drifting along the river on a summer's day, the instrumentation melds into a wash over which a lyrical guitar weaves melodies and climbs to the sky before piano chords herald a key change back into the vocal and then another of Jimmy Hastings' smoky sax outings before a piano solo punctuates the rhythm, and we leave on a reprise

of the sax. It's nine minutes in one tempo, which is a bit of a first for Caravan, and yet it suits the mood of the song, which suddenly ceases on a wave of sound.

'Head Above The Clouds' (Hastings)

'Head Above The Clouds' floats in on organ chords and viola that set an ethereal, dreamy mood before a pealing guitar heralds an uptempo tune that is driven along on a winding, melodic guitar instrumental and another straight Hastings love song. While I miss the seaside postcard humour and oddity of previous years, this more straightforward lyrical approach is indicative of a man in middle age and with a life that may not have gone quite how he imagined but has nonetheless worked out for the best. It has a lilting chorus that resolves into a guitar and synth duel where each one tries to outrun the other. Another chorus and a weaving guitar later, we hit the last verse and chorus to fade.

'Straight Through The Heart' (Hastings)

'Straight Through The Heart' has an anthemic chord sequence, which has some delicate finger picking to set a double-time rhythm over which the lead guitar punctuates the vocal lines. As odd as it may seem, this makes me think of Del Amitri – it has that Scots fascination with country-rock that runs through Celtic rock and may just be Mr Hastings reconnecting with some musical roots. It's not typical Caravan by any means, but it works beautifully.

'Wild West Street' (Hastings)

'Wild West Street' starts with windswept guitars, viola and a keyboard wash creating a soundscape in which melody is hinted at, rather than boldly stated. The soundtrack for the funeral scene in a Spaghetti Western filmed in Spain; the viola suddenly picks up a melodic line that lifts the piece and suggests walking away to a new start as the rain starts to fall. An unexpected instrumental in the middle of the songs, a change of pace, and quite sombre, stately, and lovely. A Richardson showcase, and hooray for that, as the viola had been missed up to this point.

'Nowhere To Hide' (Sinclair)

'Nowhere To Hide' starts with guest Sinclair D on piano and Geoff Richardson describing an arc of an intro and setting up the first verse. Sung by Leverton, this is a song about someone rediscovering himself and falls into the vein of writing where David Sinclair keeps things simple: the verse and chorus has a simple, catchy melody, with a great anthemic chord sequence leading to that chorus. That's twice I've used that phrase, and it's not one I would have used before: that's what's great about this band, that ability to assimilate new forms that you don't notice on first listen. Then a sudden climbing chord pattern into a glorious guitar solo that leads us back to the vocal refrain. More choppy guitar chords break up the rhythm for a keyboard solo that has sudden insertions of jazz chordings before returning to the main solo sequence – a sudden outbreak of vintage-era Caravan in the midst of the older, more mature style. Boyle delivers a jazz-rock guitar break that takes me back to hearing Alan Holdsworth in 1980 ('how does he do that?') before the keys motif returns with growling chords beneath and a sudden end. Now that's modern progressive rock!

'Linders Field' (Boyle)
Ethereal backwards guitar and flute, with a picked pattern beneath that seems regular but has sudden changes of note to catch you off-guard, takes us into Boyle's 'Linders Field', with percussion and layering of guitar and keys to create a web that the piano picks a melody across and around. Guitar fades come in and out. Atmospheric and, again, like a soundtrack, this a filmy gauze, looking through a window and seeing something that happened long, long ago...

A triumphant album. Not the progressive hippy band of *In The Land Of Grey And Pink*, nor the adult pop of *Blind Dog*..., but somewhere in between with years of living added in. That's what 36 years between the Verve album and this will do for you.

Bonus CD Tracks
'Smoking Gun (Right For Me)' (Hastings)
'The Unauthorised Breakfast Item' (Hastings)
'Tell Me Why' (Hastings)
'Revenge' (Hastings)
'For Richard' (Hastings/Coughlan/Sinclair/Sinclair)
There was a limited edition live disc with the first pressings, which had versions of 'Smoking Gun (Right For Me)', 'The Unauthorised Breakfast Item', 'Tell Me Why' and 'Revenge' recorded live in Japan which have nothing to add to the studio versions, as they had been well played-in by this point, and the obligatory 'For Richard' which was recorded in Quebec, and is perhaps of note as it does show what this line-up could do with the piece that is ultimately the test of all Caravan line-ups. And it's worth hearing simply as the band were about to go on that aforementioned hiatus before returning minus a guitarist and with a new drummer (sort of).

Paradise Filter (Caravan 2013)

Personnel:
Pye Hastings: guitar, vocal
Jan Schelhaas: keyboards, vocal
Mark Walker: drums
Jim Leverton: bass, vocal
Geoffrey Richardson: viola, violin, cello, mandolin, flute, guitar, backing vocals
Producer: Julian Gordon-Hastings
Recorded at Canterbury Sound Studios, Womenswold, 2013; released 2013
No chart placing.

With the discovery that Richard Coughlan's illness was progressive and would lead to an inability to perform with any consistency (rheumatoid arthritis causing incremental joint damage and also inclined to flare up with flu-like and debilitating symptoms almost at will), it was decided to put the band on hiatus in 2005. The idea being that they wouldn't call it a day but would leave open the possibility of gigging and maybe even recording that could be worked around Richard's illness. Of course, unpredictable as it was, this never really came to pass, and so it looked very much like the band would simply fade away. Hastings went about his business, Coughlan continued with his pub as his health would allow, and Geoff Richardson and Jim Leverton returned to the world of sessions as well as recording as a duo. Jan Schelhaas took the opportunity to record and release a solo album, which emerged in 2008. Doug Boyle found that his work was taking him elsewhere, and he officially left in 2007, knowing that any call from the band could not be guaranteed to be answered.

And that, it seemed, was that. However, just at ITV had pulled the band back from permanent retirement in 1990 with *Bedrock*, and so kick-started the last fifteen years, so in 2010 they rescued the band once more from retirement. There had been sporadic attempts to try and put together some arrangements for gigging (just two years before, a drummer of my acquaintance had been talking about the possibility of rehearsing as a stand-by drummer for some dates, which had come to nought), but it needed the spur of an invitation that would be the recognition that someone at the broadcaster thought the band deserved.

The ITV *Classic Rock Legends* series, recorded at Metropolis Studios in London, was a little better thought out than the *Bedrock* series: the recording was better, it was in front of a specially invited audience, and there were interview sections as well as a live performance. The subsequent CD and DVD are not essential and are mentioned in the live section, but it is worth dwelling here on the company in which Caravan were included. Bill Nelson and Roy Harper featured; solo artists who had in their own ways been reinventing themselves and forging forwards for years; The Zombies, these days being Rod Argent and Colin Blunstone, finally gaining the kudos that *Odessey And Oracle* had deserved; Van Der Graaf Generator, reformed for the third time and still as spiky and vital as ever; and John Lees' Barclay James Harvest (BJH being split between Lees' line-up and Les Holroyd's for some years), who were enjoying a new lease of life as a recording as well as a live act.

These were artists who had constantly been evolving through their incarnations: more importantly, they had still been active through the last few years, where Caravan had been silent. It was recognition long deserved to be asked, but it demanded that they be up to scratch. Thus, it was decided that a new drummer was required. Richard Coughlan was there and played in part, but the onus was on the new man. Mark Walker was the choice, and unlike other members of the band, he didn't come with a rock session and touring background.

Younger than the rest of the band, Walker was a journalist for professional drum magazines and had also recorded many drum tutorials. A skilled professional, he had been the pit drummer in the West End production of *The Lion King* and had been in the house band for British comedian Jack Dee's chat show. He is also part of a motivational programme called Talking Drums, which is used for inspirational events using drumming workshops and is also part of Drum Waiters, who are – as the name may suggest – waiters who are drummers and combine the two at events and promotions. A busy man with a wide range of interests and the kind of interesting character who would fit in well with the gently eccentric Caravan. A very good drummer, too, who could work to the style of Richard Coughlan without trying to copy it and could add something of his own multi-faceted style.

A great choice. The evening itself saw Coughlan put in an appearance, and he continued to play alongside Walker and also turn up to support even if unable to play.

The following year, the band played the High Voltage festival in London, sponsored by *Classic Rock* magazine, and this signalled they were back in business as a going concern. They continued to gig and made plans for recording a new album. This time, they would not rely on a label: the business models that bands such as themselves could use had changed, thanks to the continued evolution of the internet. Pioneered in this sphere by Marillion, the idea of crowdfunding and tapping your fan base so that they would pay for their album in advance, allowing you to bring in the money to record and manufacture that album, was a real option. Caravan went through the Pledgemusic site with a budget and a plan, and it must have been more than gratifying to find that their request was fulfilled by fans to the degree of 146%: a sign that Caravan fans have a deep love for the band, and trusted in whatever they would do next, musically.

Sadly, this was not to be with Richard Coughlan on board in any capacity. Worsening health had caused him to call it a day in 2012, and he sadly passed the following year. It must have been wrenching for Pye Hastings to lose his friend and musical right-hand of going on five decades, and there are moments on the subsequent album that attest to this. Come to that, Geoff Richardson had known him for four decades, and as they toured the fortieth anniversary of *For Girls Who Grow Plump In The Night* in 2013, it must have been filled with poignant moments.

Despite the sadness involved, the album – their latest studio recording of new material to date – saw a continuation of that theme of adult pop with wit, literacy, and imagination, both in the writing, the arrangement, and the performance. As we are about to see.

'All This Could Be Yours' (Hastings)

'All This Could Be Yours' begins with an organ chord, a grumbling bass, and the crashing in of guitar and drums. A simple chord sequence over which Hastings bemoans the impoverishment of modern life with an ironic chorus line. Wittily observational about the decline of a society that had once promised so much, it can be seen as a grumpy old man complaining, but the fact is that Hastings has always been a mostly optimistic writer and is from the generation that wanted to make the world better – if anyone could ask these questions, it's someone like Hastings. Musically, Schelhaas drops orchestral chords in the background and then Geoff Richardson comes in with a wonderful melancholic viola line. Leverton and Walker slot together like the drummer had always been there. The style is different, but it's a perfect fit.

'I'm On My Way' (Hastings)

'I'm On My Way' starts with a bluesy guitar riff, and the band kick in with some nice chords from Schelhaas to add tension before Hastings – the sole songwriter this time around – tells a tale of love lost and moving on. It motors on in a Chris Rea/Dire Straits manner before the melody takes a twist and Hastings reveals his intention to get some sun by the sea, at which point Richardson delivers a deft guitar solo that meanders around the melody and back into the chorus. Schelhaas then delivers a keyboard solo that is pure Caravan and takes us back forty years and links the old and new before the guitar winds up the song.

'Fingers In The Till' (Hastings)

'Fingers In The Till' starts with gentle, choral keys before Hastings begins a story of anger at someone committing fraud. Some harmonies on the chorus of this mid-paced tune sweeten the anger which comes through the lyrics. Some nice, subtle drum work on the second verse break up the arrangement before the next chorus. Richardson's guitar bubbles up underneath the vocal to take a soaring and spiralling solo to bridge to the next chorus and then plays beneath as the rhythm guitar crashes on the beat and reminds you suddenly what a good rhythm guitarist Hastings is – so good that it is only occasionally that you hear something that gives notice of how much he has been powering the songs from beneath.

'This Is What We Are' (Hastings)

'This Is What We Are' has a stuttering piano figure which is echoed by a guttural rhythm guitar, before the band kick into a song that has a straightforward verse before the stuttering rhythms break up the next verse and then a chorus that is about being individual, being true to what you are and what you do despite whatever may be going around. It seems to me that Hastings has put more obvious messages into his songs as he gets older, perhaps from exasperation at how metaphors and allegories have been missed. You can also read this song as a statement of intent. Whatever happens next for an ageing band, this is how it is. An off-the-wall guitar solo that is not like any other guitar lines so far in sound or melodic construction only serves to emphasise this point.

'Dead Man Walking' (Hastings)

'Dead Man Walking', up next, starts with a sweep of desolate Western guitars, like 'Wild West Street' with a lyric attached, this time concerning a murderer who has never let go of youthful 'eye for an eye' morality and now finds themselves reaping the consequences. A death row song, and a comment on how – whatever the crime – such things are accepted. Do we make the right choices, even if the killer has not? Viola lines punctuate the driving, almost country-rock rhythm, which is perfect for the dusty, windswept and deserted feel of the instrumental sections, where acoustic picking, dropped-in piano, and some emphatic bass notes from Leverton weave a web of tense sound and melody that echo the previous album's instrumental, Schelhaas emerging from this with a driving piano solo that rages over the rhythm section, organ swelling beneath like a toiling sea of emotion. The extended instrumental coda is superb and ends with a rattle of percussion that leads us into the next song...

'Farewell My Old Friend' (Hastings)

'Farewell My Old Friend', with piano and distant strings, is an emotional tribute to the departed Richard Coughlan, and there isn't really much to say about a song that has a heartfelt lyric that is sung with a strength that Hastings' delicate voice does not usually carry. An elegiac viola solo continues the theme when the verses end. It's quite beautiful, and a fitting goodbye. I find myself getting quite emotional listening to it, as the music of which Richard was a part has been in my life since 1977 when I was only thirteen. That's a lot of life experience with that music in the background. Can you miss someone you've never known? At a remove, perhaps.

'Pain In The Arse' (Hastings)

Of course, being Caravan, you can't be that sombre for long (and would Coughlan have wanted it any other way?) and so the next track is 'Pain In The Arse', which harks back to the Wilde Flowers' soul band roots with a Booker T and the MGs soul punch that powers a song about someone who is exactly what the title suggests, Hastings railing at them for their selfish stupidity, before a distorted viola saws in for the solo, which is extended over the chorus before Hastings returns, with some organ vamping to herald his entrance. Schelhaas trills and sweeps across his keyboard underneath a lyric that uses wit and invective to slaughter its subject. An unexpected left turn, and all the better for it.

'Trust Me I'm A Doctor' (Hastings)

'Trust Me I'm A Doctor' is a hark back to something like 'The Dog, The Dog...' and mixes humour and some double entendre in a song about a friend of the singer who is an eccentric and possibly dubious character but loveable. The accompaniment is simple and direct, as the lyric and melody are the key here: this is the type of song Hastings hadn't committed to tape for many a year and takes me back to that comment about him being able to write such humorous tunes in any era: a 1930s music hall or vaudeville could have benefitted from such a song – although the sudden chord sequence change and guitar solo that come in at the end are a pleasant surprise, seemingly having come in from another song just to make their point, which they do, with pleasure.

'I'll Be There For You' (Hastings)

'I'll Be There For You' is the penultimate track, and yet another change of mood as a delicate ballad with a splendid hook gives us another of Hastings' heartfelt love songs, with some lovely mandolin accompaniment from Richardson. Geoffrey has taken the majority of solos on this album, as he does with the mandolin break, but it must be said that these are not isolated from the rest of the band performance. As they prove when they swell up on the chorus, this is a band that is pulling in the same direction, with all performances dedicated to serving the music as a whole. This has, more often than not, been the Caravan ethos, and this track is emphatic proof of this as the band move to the end of the song with a strong piece of ensemble playing.

'The Paradise Filter' (Hastings)

And so the final song, the title track, which is introduced by a slow drum roll and some hazy chords with a whistled melody, and a Richardson vocal that is as hazy as the feel of the song itself, which is about ... er, to be honest, I'm not sure, but when he sings about putting a smile on your face in that old Cathedral town and Schelhaas delivers a vintage solo that quotes from the past before a flute joins in, you start to think that this is about the joys of being in such a band for so long, and the life it has given, and is also another, less obvious tribute, to the departed drummer. It fades out with a whistle solo that has a vague echo of the flute at the end of 'Golf Girl' and is a lovely and fitting end to what may turn out to be a valedictory album.

   If it is, then what a way to end.

The Back Catalogue Songs (Caravan 2014)

Personnel:
Pye Hastings: guitar, vocal
Mark Walker: drums
Jim Leverton: bass, vocal
Jan Schelhaas: keyboards, vocal
Geoffrey Richardson: viola, flute, percussion
Producer: Julian Hastings
Recorded Canterbury Sound Studios, Womenswold 2013; released Feb 2014;
No chart placing.
From the album sleeve: 'Dedicated to the memory of Richard Coughlan 1947-2013.'

The following year, the band went into the studio again, this time to put down some classic Caravan tunes and so record how they performed them live. To this end, they recorded the set as if live, with no dubbing. To date, it's the last time that they have been in the studio. Live performances have been sporadic, and some dates have been completed with depping musicians (such as John Etheridge, who stood in during some Spanish dates) when calendars have clashed. The band have continued and intend to do so when 'normal' life is resumed after the pandemic that decimated 2020 in so many ways.

In the meantime, Pye Hastings finally got to record that solo album after so many years and false starts. Thanks to another Pledgemusic campaign *From The Half House* was recorded and released in 2017. With Pye handling guitar and bass as well as vocals, the drums were supplied by Mark Walker and the keys by near(ish) neighbour in Scotland (where Pye now resides) Jan Schelhaas. Of course, sax and flute are added by brother Jimmy, who is still playing. The songs are a little different to Caravan tunes in arrangement and feel and mine the more straightforward pop and rock styles that Pye has used in the band. Not that this has stopped them from adding one or two of these to their set since 2018, mind.

With all the members of the band still active musically, there is little doubt that Caravan will carry on until too infirm to carry a guitar or climb on stage; the only obstacles will be arranging those calendars.

But for now, the last statement we have is this 'live in the studio' recording of some classics. It seems a bit anti-climactic and pointless until you consider some of the live releases mentioned further on, some of which were not sanctioned and are from the last twenty years, poorly recorded and presented, and not representing the band at their best.

So, what we have here is the current line-up recording classics from the early years of the band as they perform them now.

'Memory Lain, Hugh / Headloss' (Hastings)
'For Richard' (Hastings/Coughlan/Sinclair/Sinclair)
'Memory Lain, Hugh / Headloss' has not changed much in essence, though the energy of the second half is slightly diminished by the years, and the opening

riff is more of a shuffle than hitherto; and to tackle 'For Richard' is obligatory. In this version, Walker shows his delicacy of technique as a drummer, and without Boyle's extra guitar, the riff section is not so lead guitar-dominated. This is the first recorded version without Richard Coughlan behind the kit, and to say that it doesn't seem to matter is a testament to Walker's skills.

'Nine Feet Underground' (Hastings/Coughlan/Sinclair/Sinclair)

'Nine Feet Underground' here runs for seventeen minutes instead of the original's 22 minutes, with some of the keyboard soloing and the final mad charging riff section truncated. It doesn't matter, and it is nice to hear Leverton properly on 'Disassociation', as he has made it his own, and a dyed-in-the-wool Sinclair R fan like myself would never have imagined saying that once upon a time.

'The Dog, The Dog, He's At It Again' (Hastings)
'In The Land Of Grey And Pink' (Hastings/Coughlan/Sinclair/ Sinclair)

'The Dog, The Dog, He's At It Again' and 'In The Land Of Grey And Pink' are not obvious choices, but they are capably handled – the harmonies in the former have always been a problem live as it's never been possible to reproduce that, but a bit of clever ensemble rearrangement handles that problem. In the latter, much as with the '90s cottage industry remake, a deft piece of rearrangement to shape the song to Hastings' voice removes the spectre of Richard Sinclair from looming over the rendition.

An odd release on which to end this section, as it's live and it's old material – very old, actually – but yet it looks forward to the future as it showcases how the band view their past and how they approach their craft now that they are men who (Walker aside) should be collecting their pensions and not hitting the road once more.

Conclusion

In a sense, this sums Caravan up: looking back but moving forward, as they have at every stage in their history. The music that has come before defines how they were and informs what is to come: but it's what is to come that is always more important to them.

BBC Recordings

BBC Radio One Live In Concert (Windsong 1991)

'Introduction'
'The Love In Your Eye'
'For Richard'
'The Dabsong Conshirtoe'
'Hoedown'

This was recorded in 1975 and is liberally plundered for other BBC archive discs. Recorded at the Paris Theatre London on 21 March 1975, it features the Hastings/Coughlan/Sinclair/Richardson/Wedgewood line-up and has an early outing for the Sinclair/Murphy '...Conshirtoe', albeit in a slightly shorter form. It's a common thing in these live and BBC releases for both '...Conshirtoe' and 'Nine Feet...' to be truncated in some form. This is partly because when playing live, the band ups the pace, and partly because – particularly in the former case – some of the studio effects and trickery have to be cut out and substituted by a swift bit of rearranging.

Like all the 'In Concert' and live shows that the BBC specially arranged and recorded in the '70s and '80s, these are concerts where the band works to a shorter set-list rather than playing the regular set and being edited after the fact or faded out. As a result, whenever you hear any sets from that era, they have an intense focus. That applies here, where you can see that Wedgewood's presence has toughened the band's sound so that they have more of an edge than they did with John G Perry – which is no slight, as Perry is a fine player with a jazzier edge than Wedgewood that means the music was less rock-driven with him in place.

It's a strong set list and a good performance. Its essential nature is only diluted by the fact that its tracks have been spread over other releases and that the Fairfield Halls full live set was eventually released, giving an even better picture of Caravan live in this period. Its benefit over the Nottingham release is good old BBC engineering – they had some great recording engineers in this period.

Songs For Oblivion Fishermen (Hux 1998)

'Hello, Hello'
'If I Could Do It All over Again, I'd Do It All Over You'
'As I Feel I Die'
'Love Song Without Flute'
'Love To Love You'
'In The Land Of Grey And Pink'
'Memory Lain, Hugh'
'A Hunting We Shall Go / Backwards '
'The Love In Your Eye'
'Mirror For The Day'

'For Richard'
'Virgin On The Ridiculous'

Recorded live for the BBC:
Tracks 1-3: *Top Of The Pops* on 19 August 1970
Tracks 4-6: Alan Black on 11 March 1971, transmitted on 9 April 1971
Tracks 7,8: John Peel on 20 August 1973, transmitted on 30 August 1973
Tracks 9-12: John Peel on 7 February 1974, transmitted on 14 February 1974

The first six tracks feature the Hastings/Coughlan/Sinclair/Sinclair line-up, while the latter six have the Hastings/Coughlan/Sinclair/Richardson/Perry line-up

The first six, as with many live recordings of this line-up scattered on TV and radio, show that the first line-up, while capable of feyness and whimsy on record, still retained their beat and psychedelic roots when it came to bashing it out live or in a couple of takes. These are slightly harder-edged versions of these tunes and give the younger listener a chance to feel what it may have been like to see the original line-up at the time.

The second six are much more polished; though shorn of the extra instrumentation that exists on the studio versions, we can hear how Sinclair and Richardson filled those gaps with extra flourishes, and it also gives a rare chance to actually hear how much John G Perry contributed in his short time in the band – backing vocals are up a notch (David is not a great singer, and I always thought Pye and Richard's voices tended to block each other out in the mid-range), and there is some lovely supple bass playing on show here.

Ether Way (Hux 1998)
'The Show Of Our Lives'
'Stuck In A Hole'
'The Dabsong Conshirtoe'
'All The Way'
'A Very Smelly Grubby Little Oik / Bobbing Wide / Come On Back / Grubby Oik Reprise'
'Behind You'
'The Last Unicorn'
'Nightmare'
'Better By Far'
Recorded live for the BBC:
Tracks 1-3: for John Peel at Maida Vale Studio 6, London, England on 26 June 1975, transmitted on 3 July 1975
Tracks 4-5: for John Peel at Maida Vale Studio 4, London, England on 6 May 1976, transmitted on 17 May 1976
Tracks 6-9: for John Peel at Maida Vale Studio 4, London, England on 2 May 1977, transmitted on 10 May 1977

The first three tracks feature the Hastings/Coughlan/Sinclair/Wedgewood/ Richardson line-up; on tracks 4 & 5, David Sinclair is replaced by Jan Schelhaas, and then from tracks 6-9 Mike Wedgewood departs, replaced by Dek Messecar.

It's another bloody awful cover from Hux, but who cares when they manage to unearth something like this. Personally, this is my favourite BBC release for the simple reason that – for all the faults and stumbles in the latter part of the '70s – I still think that *Blind Dog...* and *Better By Far* are under-rated and deserve more credit than they would get. And the sessions featuring that line-up, and songs from those albums, prove it to my ears.

As an aside, it still seems odd to see John Peel giving sessions to a band like Caravan in 1977, given his volte-face to punk and after, dropping virtually everything that came before.

For the *Cunning Stunts*-period songs, we have strong, driven performances that echo the 'In Concert' strengths of the same era. These three will crop up again very shortly.

So, we come to the real meat of the release. The songs from *Blind Dog* are harder-edged in the case of the 'Oik' sequence, which really highlights what a great riff-powered tune that is. Meanwhile, on 'Taking It All The Way', Geoffrey excels on the viola. This is probably one of my favourite Hastings songs, as mentioned at length, and this is a great version.

The last four tracks are from *Better By Far* and to me, highlight what is lacking in the album. We have good songs, albeit more mainstream rock and pop than hitherto, and here they sparkle and have a grit that is missing in the too-polite studio versions. There's also more bottom end, and as you know, my complaint about the last three studio albums in the first era was that they lacked a bottom end and were too thin and toppy. They benefit immensely from this.

Mind you, you wouldn't necessarily think that 'Nightmare' and 'The Last Unicorn' would need this, but again they benefit from tight studio session time and have more of a spark in the playing because of that live adrenaline feel. The latter is perhaps the last full-blown 'prog' outing for the band, albeit in just six minutes, and possibly points the way to where Richardson was headed next.

Green Bottles For Marjorie (The Lost BBC Sessions)
(Caravan 2004)
'Green Bottles For Marjorie'
'Place Of My Own'
'Feelin' Reelin' Squealin''
'Ride'
'Nine Feet Underground'
'In The Land Of Grey And Pink'
'Feelin' Reelin' Squealin''
'The Love In Your Eye'
Previously lost sessions recorded for the BBC:

Tracks 1-4: John Peel's *Top Gear* show at Maida Vale Studio 4, London, England on 31 December 1968, first broadcast on 5 January 1969
Tracks 5-7: *Radio One In Concert*, recorded and first broadcast on 16 May 1971
Track 8: John Peel's show at Maida Vale Studio 4, London, England on 11 April 1972, first broadcast on 2 May 1972

This is either a treasure or an annoyance, depending on how you feel about hi-fidelity. These were lost session recordings, 'found' in the sense that someone who had taped them off the radio many years back made sure that the tape found its way to a semi-official release. If you don't mind lo-fi, it's a marvellous discovery: but it is distinctly muffled and muddy and might frustrate those with a higher threshold for sound quality.

Having said that, we have a series of songs that mostly come from the early days, with the first line-up. 'Green Bottles...' itself is not a lost song, but rather an early version of 'If I Could Do It Again, I'd Do It All Over You' with a different lyric in places. 'Feelin' Reelin' Squealin' ' is a cover of the first Soft Machine single, and to be honest, Caravan make a better job of it (but then I'm not really keen on the Softs until *Third*, so don't take that as gospel). It has a free-form freakout section and shows they could rock with the best of them.

The exception is the last track, which is an excellent version of the track from *Waterloo Lily*, with Steve Miller on keyboards rather than David Sinclair. The song turns up again in a better quality recording on 'The Show Of Our Lives', but that's a later session with David Sinclair. It's very different in feel, and as such, I'll take this opportunity to posit that it does show here, more than on the album they made with that line-up, why it was inevitable that Miller and Sinclair would soon depart. Steve had been invited to join by Richard after he had played with Steve and his brother Phil, who had just finished with Delivery. Phil was in his brief tenure with Matching Mole, and both brothers relished freedom in their playing, which their subsequent careers demonstrated. This was something Richard also seemed keen to embrace, but here in stark miniature, and on the studio album as a whole, you can hear that the free camp and the more arranged and song-based intentions of Messrs Hastings and Coughlan are pulling against each other. That dynamic tension is why the album has very high points, and some aimless ambling points: it could never work long-term, but in truth, some of the best pure playing in Caravan occurs on that album and is demonstrated in this track.

The Show Of Our Lives – Caravan At The BBC 1968-75
(Deram 2007)
CD One
'Place Of My Own'
'Ride'
'If I Could Do It All Over Again, I'd Do It All Over You'
'Hello, Hello'

'As I Feel I Die'
'Love To Love You'
'Love Song Without Flute'
'In The Land Of Grey And Pink'
'Nine Feet Underground'
'Feelin', Reelin', Squealin''
'A Hunting We Shall Go Waffle Part One: Be Alright & Chance Of A Lifetime'

CD Two
'Memory Lain, Hugh'
'Headloss'
'The Love In Your Eye'
'Mirror For The Day'
'Virgin On The Ridiculous'
'For Richard'
'The Dabsong Conshirtoe'
'Stuck In A Hole'
'The Show Of Our Lives'

Tracks 1,2: John Peel's *Top Gear* show at Maida Vale Studio 4, London, England on 31 December 1968, first broadcast on 5 January 1969
Tracks 3-5: BBC Transcription Service *Top Of* The *Pops* on 19 August 1970
Tracks 6-8: *Sounds Of The Seventies* on 11 March 1971
Tracks 9,10: John Peel's *Sunday Concert* at The Paris Theatre, London, England on 6 May 1971
Tracks 11-14: *In Concert* at The Paris Theatre, London, England on 2 August 1973
Tracks 15-18: John Peel's Radio show on 7 February 1974, first broadcast on 14 February 1974
Track 19: *In Concert* at The Paris Theatre, London, England on 21 March 1975
Tracks 20,21: John Peel's Radio show at Maida Vale Studio 6, London, England on 26 June 1975, first broadcast on 3 July 1975

So, here we have a collection that takes the best of the BBC tapes that had previously been released, omitting the muddier early takes and ignoring the session material from the BTM/Arista years (it is on Decca, after all). This is the best all-round collection of BBC material and the easiest to get hold of: the two tracks that appeared on *Green Bottles* have been cleaned up and still sound lo-fi, but distinctly less muddy. There's a different version of 'Feelin' Reelin' Squealin'' that loses nothing of the energy of the earlier version, and the line-ups with Richardson, Perry and Wedgewood show that without the freer jazz leanings of Richard Sinclair, Caravan as a live band had become rawer, and had more of an edge on the tighter, rockier sections of their music, while still able to soften and reflect the romantic edge that infused their melodies. Just listen to the tracks on Disc Two, particularly the first three, and you realise that where Sinclair R and Miller S had joined temporary forces in Hatfield And The North (before Steve left to pursue an even more free jazz path) to play a freer music, they would never have been able to stick to the kind of discipline needed to play the music from *For Girls*. Listen to that album and the first Hatfields album, and you know that both parties made the right decision (and gave us even more excellent music, by the way). The discipline to stick to tight arrangements is a long way from the kind of discipline needed by the dedicated free player.

Live Recordings
Live: Canterbury Comes To London (Transatlantic 1999)
'Memory Lain, Hugh'
'Headloss'
'Nine Feet Underground'
'The Dog, The Dog, He's At It Again'
'Cold As Ice'
'Somewhere In Your Heart'
'I Know Why You're Laughing'
'Liar'
'For Richard'
'Golf Girl'

This was recorded at the Astoria, London, in May 1997 and features the Hastings/Coughlan/Richardson/Sinclair/Leverton/Boyle/Bentall line-up. It has a good mix of Caravan classics and some songs that were new at the time. Doug Boyle, in particular, puts in a good performance, though I did always wonder if there was enough space in the music for both Boyle and Richardson. Certainly, there isn't much room to breathe as the arrangements can seem a little cluttered live. However, that should not detract from what is a strong live document of a re-invigorated band. And it has to be said that while vocally Jim Leverton is no Richard Sinclair (who is?), he has always made a good fist of his vocal section of 'Nine Feet Underground' – the bassist's bit, basically – and over time has made it his own in a live setting. As a document of a reawakening band, this is actually a bit of a vital release.

Surprise Supplies (HTD 1999)
'Here Am I'
'Chiefs And Indians'
'Can You Hear Me?'
'All The way (With John Wayne's Single-Handed Liberation Of Paris)'
'A Very Smelly Grubby Little Oik / Bobbing Wide / Come On Back / Love In Your Eye /To Catch Me A Brother / Sub Sultus / Débouchement / Tilbury Kecks'

Another live release in 1999, but this is of an earlier vintage and is also well worth tracking down, being as it is one of the few documents of how the *Blind Dog*-era band sounded on stage. This is the Hastings/Coughlan/Richardson/Wedgewood/Schelhaas line-up, recorded on 5 May 1976 at the New Victoria Theatre in London. On the night, they were augmented by Jimmy Hastings, on sax/clarinet/flute, and that is what makes this just that little bit special. 'Chiefs And Indians' and 'All The Way' benefitted immensely on vinyl from the added presence of the elder Hastings, and to have him trapped on tape performing live with the band is a little bit special. I make no bones about the fact that *Blind Dog* is up there with *Grey And Pink* as my favourite Caravan albums, so

I am biased. Those who prefer the earlier records, or like the current line-up live and on record, may well disagree with my verdict here. But for me, this is a strong line-up promoting an album that followed *Cunning* Stunts into the charts and seemed to indicate a new commercial era for the band.

We know that it didn't pan out that way, but there is an optimism and fire in the band that lifts this up as a performance, and the choice of material is interesting. Obviously, it concentrates on the new album, but the 'Love In Your Eye' cycle is perhaps unexpected: what it does is give Jan Schelhaas a chance to stretch out, and show he is the equal of David Sinclair and Steve Miller when it comes to the ivories, which is something that the more song-based and tighter material Pye Hastings was writing did not necessarily allow.

Live At Fairfield Halls 1974 (Decca 2002)
'Memory Laine, Hugh / Headloss'
'Virgin On The Ridiculous'
'Be Alright / Chance Of A Lifetime'
'The Love In Your Eye'
'L'Auberge Du Sanglier / A Hunting We Shall Go'
'The Dog, The Dog, He's At It Again'
'For Richard'
'Hoedown'

Now here's a live album with a history to it. For a start, it was Mike Wedgewood's first gig with the band, which is perhaps not the best way to ease someone in: 'By the way, Mike, we're recording this for a possible live release, so no pressure...'

But from there, it gets more complicated. 'For Richard' snuck out first as an unreleased tempter to get existing fans to buy the 1976 *Canterbury Tales* compilation (see further on). It's a cracking performance and left you wanting more from the first fruits of the Hastings/Coughlan/Richardson/Wedgewood/Sinclair line-up.

Which you weren't going to get unless you were French. That's right: only the French were privy to the 1980 release *The Best Of Caravan – Live*, which was Terry King's attempt to try and cash in on / follow up *The Album*, as the band had once again splintered in the face of mass apathy in the UK. It was a reasonable move, given that the French were always a strong market for the band, but to call it *The Best Of* given the track listing, was not going to endear it to some people. Which may be why it was never released anywhere else.

And so, the tapes drifted into abeyance, only to be plundered for the Canterbury *Tales* reissue/revamp in the '90s (see further on, again). A frustrating glimpse of what you couldn't hear (unless you were French and had the vinyl double squirreled away). Which was a crying shame, as the performances that had been heard were excellent, as was the recording and mixing quality.

And then it was suddenly released out of the blue by Decca, partly because of their reissue programme of Caravan albums (not just Caravan, Universal were plundering the Decca archives for anything progressive at this point), and partly perhaps because the reformed band had steadily rebuilt and enhanced their fan base since the mid 90s. No matter why, the fact is that we were now able to hear the full set (almost – no 'Chance Of A Lifetime', which was played that night and not very often otherwise).

Was it worth the wait? Yes, frankly: from the moment that Richardson's viola hums and drones with tension under the opening chords, it's obvious that this was a re-energised line-up with something to prove. New bassist, new ideas (as would soon be seen), and new management: and frankly, it sounds like a band about to embark on what they saw as a new beginning. The playing is energised and tight while at the same time allowing enough room for interplay between the lead instruments that shows just enough spontaneity to keep things fresh and on edge. Driving it is a rhythm section where Coughlan responds to the harder rock pulse of Wedgewood's playing: this is less jazzy and swinging than before, without losing any limber.

'Virgin On The Ridiculous' is a revelation shorn of the orchestral accompaniment that listeners were used to from the 'New Symphonia' album, and to top it all the harmonies and round singing on 'The Dog, The Dog, He's At It Again' are exceptionally strong, which they have to be shorn of the album version's multi-tracking.

It was a release hinted at and teased with for decades, but worth the wait. Of course, it was only in print for three years, so finding it may not be that easy (again) – but well worth the effort.

A Hunting We Shall Go: Live in 1974 (Vivid 2008)
'A Hunting We Shall Go'
'For Richard'
'Hoedown'

Short but not so sweet. Again, this is the Hastings/Coughlan/Richardson/Wedgewood/Sinclair line-up, captured on the same tour as the Fairfield Halls recording, but in a more truncated form and with not so much fidelity. There's nothing wrong with the playing on this release, but it doesn't give you many variations in material, and you're hearing it in a muddier mix. Also, you have to question the intelligence that goes into a release like this. You get three songs and just a tad over half an hour running time. On a CD. Does this mean there was nothing else recorded at that time that could be licensed, or purely that the licensee thought it might be a wheeze to chop a set in half and then, if this one sold ok, to bang out another half-hour release? Honestly, it does make you wonder, and it's a shame, as the band were really on form during this tour. I've included it as it has curio value, but you're much better off tracking down the Fairfield Halls concert. Or even...

Live UK Tour 1975 (Koch MLP 2003)
'Show Of Our Lives'
'Memory Lain, Hugh'
'Headloss'
'Dabsong Conshirtoe'
'Virgin On The Ridiculous'
'Be Alright'
'Chance Of A Lifetime'
'Love In Your Eye'
'For Richard'

Actually, fair play, as a companion to Fairfield Halls would be more accurate. This was recorded for ATV at Nottingham Polytechnic on 5 December 1975 and would see the band swapping keyboard players. David Sinclair was gone, and in was Jan Schelhaas to join the Hastings/Coughlan/Richardson/Wedgewood team. By now, the rhythm section had gelled, and both Pye and Geoff were playing to their strengths. By contrast, the keyboards are competent and good, but there is no flash and no attempt to shine (contrast this with the set a year later on *Surprise Supplies*). It's a strong ensemble set, but whereas the interplay between Sinclair and Richardson had developed to a kind of jousting, here it's very much the Geoff Richardson show, as he shoulders the burden while Schelhaas beds in. To be fair, with Steve Miller being there and gone in the blink of an eye, Schelhaas was basically stepping into the shoes of the man who had to a great degree defined the Caravan sound, so it's no wonder he started cautiously. That wouldn't last.

The sound quality here is good but lacks a punch. TV recording engineers back in the '70s were not always geared up for recording live rock bands. Having said that, it is clear and not at all muddy. These would have been ATV engineers, the franchise that later became Central. They weren't too hot in their own studios, either, as we shall see.

Caravan Live (Demon 1993)
'Headloss'
'Videos Of Hollywood'
'Nine Feet Underground'
'If I Could Do It Again, I'd Do It All Over You'
'Winter Wine'
'In The Land Of Grey And Pink'
'For Richard'

This was the first live album released, so I suppose I should have put it at the beginning of this section, but I've got it out of sequence for a reason.

So, Caravan had called it a day in 1982 after *Back To Front* sunk without trace. It seemed like they were forever consigned to the 'where are they now?' files.

But then along came Central. The Midlands ITV franchise in those days of regional TV, they had an idea to get a whole load of bands from the turn of the seventies and get them into a studio to record sets that were to be broadcast late at night. The rough theme (very rough) being that it was twenty years past their heyday. This may have been true of the bands – like Caravan – that had split but was a bit harsh on the likes of Hawkwind, Wishbone Ash, and Uriah Heep, who were all invited along. As were Gong, who had recently sort of reformed (now there's a convoluted history for you), and were at least not so bombastic and guitar-heavy as the other acts who were recorded.

The original line-up were invited, and they played a set that – as can be seen – was heavy on very early material, with 'Videos Of Hollywood' from the *Back To Front* album (one of the least 'Caravan' songs on there, so baffling) and 'Headloss' (again, a baffling choice as it was post Richard's first stint).

I remember being excited at the broadcast and then disappointed when it aired. Watching it, it seemed like Richard didn't really want to be there; Pye was ring-rusty and looked like he wanted to fade into the background, and David was using some very late 1980s kit that sounded out of place on the older material.

Hearing it since it's actually not that bad. Apart from the keyboard sounds: nothing can disguise the fact that they are of their time, and the earlier material demanded sounds and textures that they could not supply, which shouldn't detract from the usual inventive Sinclair D performance. Sinclair R may have looked like he didn't want to be there, but he certainly doesn't play like that, with very slippery and inventive bass lines. Pye does still sound ring-rusty, it has to be said: the voice, which was always fragile (its strength) sounds a little quivery at times, though his rhythm playing is immaculate as always. Mr Coughlan does what he always does, quietly, efficiently, and excellently.

The main issue is the sound quality: it lacks punch and is weak, betraying the playing. It's typical TV sound of that era and has the same pitfalls as the live set recorded by another line-up fifteen years before, hence my including it here.

Mind you, it's not like the other bands in the series fared any better with the sound, and it served none of them well. A pity, as it was a nice idea at a time when bands of this type and vintage were ignored or pilloried.

Perhaps the real importance of this night was that it opened the door for the original line-up to tour again; and even when Richard Sinclair headed for the door once more, it gave them the impetus to continue and to start thinking about new material and becoming a working band (albeit part-time) again.

A Night's Tale – Live In The USA (Classic Rock Legends 2002)
'All The Way' / 'A Very Smelly, Grubby Little Oik'
'Nine Feet Underground'
'Medley: The Dabsong Conshirtoe / All Aboard / Where But For Caravan Would I? / O Caroline / The Dabsong / The Love In Your Eye / Backwards A Hunting We Shall Go'
'Nightmare'

'I Know Why You're Laughing'
'For Richard'

One of three albums released by the Classic Rock Legends label and featuring the line-up of Coughlan/Hastings/Leverton/Boyle/Bentall/Richardson/Schelhaas. Recorded live at NEARfest, Patriots Theater, Trenton, New Jersey, USA on 29 June 2002, this has material that overlaps with the following two albums, and taken together, they overwhelmingly represent the older material in the set at that time. The performances are good, and the recording is of good quality. They are geared very much for the retro market and don't represent the new material that had been produced since the mid-1990s.

The main sticking point for these is that they have never been approved by the band or management, and while not exactly bootlegs, their release could be said to contravene the terms of the original recording. So, it's up to you if you want them or not: they're not essential, put it that way.

Nowhere To Hide (Classic Rock Legends 2002)
'All The Way' / 'A Very Smelly Grubby Little Oik'
'Liar'
'The Dog, The Dog, He's At It Again'
'Nowhere To Hide'
'Nightmare'
'For Richard'
'Memory Lain, Hugh / Headloss'
'If I Could Do It All Over Again, I'd Do It All Over You'

There's not much to add to this – as stated, it's not really official. It's a decent overview of that line-up at that time. Irritating that there are overlaps – at least they could have carved the set up so that it didn't repeat itself.

With Strings Attached (Classic Rock Legends 2002)
'Headloss'
'The Dog, The Dog, He's At It Again'
'Travelling Ways'
'Medley: The Dabsong Conshirtoe / All Aboard / Where But For Caravan Would I? / O Caroline / The Dabsong / The Love In Your Eye / Backwards / A Hunting We Shall Go'
'Nine Feet Underground'
'Nightmare'
'For Richard' (With Orchestra)

And repeat! If you combined these (and ignored the dubious nature of the release) then at least you'd have a decent set. And you get an orchestra in here as well, which is nice.

Incidentally, in the medley (repeated over two releases *sigh*) it's worth noting that the 'Dabsong' material is split into sections, and they also slip in a cover of 'O Caroline', which was written by David Sinclair with Robert Wyatt, and was the first track on the first Matching Mole album. It's an odd choice, as the original is so definitive.

You'd be much better searching out...

Recorded Live In Concert At Metropolis Studios London
(Salvo Sound And Vision 2010)
'Memory Lain, Hugh'
'Headloss'
'And I Wish I Were Stoned'
'Golf Girl'
'Smoking Gun (Right For Me)'
'The Unauthorised Breakfast Item'
'Nightmare'
'Hello, Hello'
'Give Me More'
'Fingers In The Till
I'm On My Way'
'Nine Feet Underground'

So, it's 2010 and the idea behind this was a little like the *Bedrock* format from twenty years earlier: let's get a bunch of bands who have been around forever, get them to play in front of an invited audience of long-time fans, record it for TV and audio, and do a bit of interview stuff as well. In other words, let's do it as it should have been done for *Bedrock*, and let's make sure that they have a good sound.

Which they did. This is very well recorded and finds a band that are on good form. We have Messrs Hastings, Richardson, Leverton and Schelhaas joined by new drummer Mark Walker. Richard Coughlan, though forced into retirement by his health, was also there on the day and contributed to the chat elements (does Geoffrey Richardson still encounter fans who think of him as 'the new boy'?).

Musically, the band are relaxed and in a more laid back mood, though still upping the pace and tension when the music requires it. This is a celebratory and low-key gig, though, with a small audience and Richardson on 'I even play the garden shears' form. The setlist is a trawl through all eras of the band, with some post-reformation songs, the welcome appearance of a couple of *Better By Far* tunes, some early songs, and the almost obligatory 'Memory Lain, Hugh' / 'Headloss' and 'Nine Feet Underground'. Let's be honest, playing those must be written into their tour contracts. And why not? If you want an indication of what the band has been like over the last decade, this is as good a place as any to look.

Compilations
Canterbury Tales (Decca 1976)
'If I Could Do It All Over Again, I'd Do It All Over You'
'Aristocracy'
'Can't Be Long Now / Françoise / For Richard / Warlock'
'Nine feet underground: Nigel Blows A Tune / Love's A Friend / Make It 76 /
Dance Of The Seven Paper Hankies / Hold Grandad By The Nose / Honest I Did!
/ Disassociation / 100% Proof'
'Golf Girl'
'Hoedown'
'The Love In Your Eye / To Catch Me A Brother / Subsultus / Débouchement /
Tilbury Kecks'
'Memory Lain, Hugh / Headloss'
'Virgin On The Ridiculous'
'The Dog, The Dog, He's At It Again'

Released as this was to cash-in on the band's first BTM/Arista album and
foray into the album charts, it could be seen as a bit of a spoiler or perhaps
as a primer to earlier releases. However you choose to look at it, it's a
very strong selection that covers the style changes in the band over their
Decca years whilst emphasising the continuity they maintained (mostly
through the writing of Pye Hastings). I can only assume the lack of material
from *Cunning Stunts* – annoying as that was to me back then – was on the
assumption that the latter would still be in shops, so go and buy it, kids!

It does have one track that was – at the time – very much of note. The
version of 'For Richard' here comes from the Fairfield Halls concert that
is now available in its entirety. Apart from its appearance here, it was
unavailable for years* until cropping up on the expanded reissue of
Cunning Stunts and then becoming a part of the complete concert issue.
(*Unless you got the original France-only concert issue via Kingdom, of
course!)

It was, at the time, a revelation as it presented a more muscular, raw
version of the band than the studio tracks would have you believe. By
accident or design, choosing 'For Richard' demonstrated that progress more
than perhaps any other song. The original is wispy and spectral to begin
before Jimmy Hastings' free-wheeling sax propels it into jazzier areas. With
Geoff Richardson replacing the sax with viola, it became a piece that began
almost mournfully before exploding into a riff monster that rocks while the
viola roams melodically across the top line. It was a demonstration of their
progression and how much bringing in Geoff Richardson, and latterly Mike
Wedgewood had toughened up the sound while still being able to keep the
melodic sensitivity that had marked them from the start as special.

As a thirteen-year-old, hearing it announced as a song about David
Sinclair's 'brother' – before being corrected with a self-deprecating 'I must

brush up on my Caravan history' – made me wonder why this guy knew nothing about the band he'd joined (even I knew that, if only from the sleeve notes of the very album I was listening to) ... the older me thinks this is a crafty way of drawing in the confidence of the audience.

The Show Of Our Lives (Decca 1981)
'Love To Love You (And Tonight Pigs Will Fly)'
'In The Land Of Grey And Pink'
'Golf Girl'
'Love Song Without Flute'
'The Love In Your Eye'
'If I Could Do It All over Again, I'd Do It All Over You'
'Hello, Hello'
'And I Wish I Were Stoned'
'For Richard'
'Headloss'
'The Show of Our Lives'
'Memory Lain, Hugh'

A very nice selection, the timing of which is quite odd when you look back to the period: after *The Album*, Caravan had splintered again and were only pulled back together by an 'original line-up' reunion – but that was a year away. Meanwhile, anything of this ilk was being sneered at by the music press and radio, and any potential new fans would be diverted by the plethora of new and innovative music that was springing up post-punk. As such, this was bound to sink without trace. Record executives, dontcha love 'em?

Songs And Signs (Elite 1991)
'Welcome The Day'
'Songs And Signs'
'The Love In Your Eye'
'Winter Wine'
'Mirror For The Day' (Live)
'The Show Of Our Lives'
'For Richard' (Live)
'Surprise, Surprise'
'Hello, Hello'
'The World Is Yours'

Again, nothing here that hasn't been discussed earlier. An odd release date, which is why I note it: that was when John Tracey at Decca was in the middle of his Caravan reissue programme, so why they would license material at that point is a conundrum.

Canterbury Tales – The Best Of Caravan (London 1996)
'Place Of My Own'
'Magic Man'
'Hello, Hello'
'If I Could Do It All Over Again, I'd Do It All Over You'
'And I Wish I Were Stoned / Don't Worry'
'Can't Be Long Now / Francoise / For Richard / Warlock'
'Love To Love You (And Tonight Pigs Will Fly)'
'Golf Girl'
'Nine Feet Underground'
'Songs And Signs'
'The World Is Yours'
'Memory Lain, Hugh'
'Headloss'
'The Dog, The Dog, He's At It Again'
'Be All Right / Chance Of A Lifetime'
'L'Auberge Du Sanglier / A Hunting We Shall Go / Pengola / Backwards / A Hunting We Shall Go (Reprise)'
'The Love In Your Eye' (Live)
'For Richard' (Live)
'Stuck In A Hole'
'Lover / No Backstage Pass'
'The Show Of Our Lives'

This is an expanded reissue of the earlier compilation – how strange is that, reissuing compilations? Sometimes it's hard to fathom how the minds of record company executives work. It's not as though the original albums hadn't been issued on CD just a few years before. It's a decent selection of material, with no surprises, though it is more comprehensive as it covers the Verve debut (which wasn't owned by the same company as Decca at that point) and also has some tracks from *Cunning Stunts*, which always frustrated me at the time of the original issue. Note also a couple more of the Fairfield Halls live tracks get an outing before the whole set was finally issued (properly – as detailed previously).

Travelling Man (Mooncrest 1998)
'In The Land Of Grey And Pink'
'The Crack Of The Willow'
'Cold As Ice'
'Liar'
'If I Could Do It All over Again, I'd Do It All Over You'
'Cool Water'
'Travelling Ways'
'Place of My Own'

'Somewhere In Your Heart'
'Wendy Wants Another 6" Mole'
'Side By Side'
'I Know Why You're Laughing'
'If It Wasn't for Your Ego'
'It's a Sad, Sad Affair'

This is not to be confused with the later *Travelling Ways*, though the same comments apply (read on to see). At the end of the day, an alternative way to pick up some HTD era tracks as the original releases may be elusive.

The Show Of Our Lives (Mooncrest 1998)
'Love To Love You (And Tonight Pigs Will Fly)'
'In The Land Of Grey And Pink'
'Golf Girl'
'Love Song Without Flute'
'Love In Your Eye'
'If I Could Do It All Over Again, I'd Do It All Over You'
'Hello, Hello'
'And I Wish I Were Stoned'
'For Richard'
'Headloss'
'The Show Of Our Lives'
'Memory Lain, Hugh'

And here we are with another Mooncrest comp from the same year, except this time it's all licensed from Universal/Decca and is classic period rather than reformed era. Which, as two companion volumes, makes a kind of sense – except that neither is really well labelled and there's no link between them to alert or tempt the buyer of one with the existence of the other. I suppose it was okay as an option before the CD reissues of the original albums happened, though.

Headloss (Delta Music 1999)
'Asforteri'
'Cool Water'
'Don't Want Love'
'Golf Girl'
'Headloss' (Live at London Astoria)
'Hello, Hello'
'If I Could Do It All Over Again, I'd Do It All Over You'
'In The Land Of Grey And Pink'
'Nine Feet Underground' (Live at London Astoria)
'This Time'
'To The Land Of My Fathers'

Another seemingly aimless compilation, but of note as 'Headloss' and 'Nine Feet Underground' are live recordings from the Astoria. I stand to be corrected, but they sound like they're taken from *Canterbury Comes To London*. I've included this in case my ears are wrong.

Travelling Ways: The HTD Anthology (Castle 2001)

'It's A Sad, Sad Affair'
'Cold As Ice'
'Somewhere In Your Heart'
'This Time'
'If It Wasn't for You Ego'
'Wendy Wants Another 6" Mole'
'I Know Why You're Laughing'
'If I Could Do It All Over Again, I'd Do It All Over You'
'Place of My Own'
'In The Land Of Grey And Pink'
'Golf Girl'
'Hello, Hello'
'Asforteri'
'Memory Lain, Hugh'
'Be All Right / Chance Of A Lifetime'
'Headloss' (Live)
'Liar' (Live)
'For Richard' (Live)
'Travelling Ways' (Live)
'Hoedown'
'The Dog, The Dog, He's At It Again'
'Stuck in a Hole'
'Ride'
'C'thlu Thlu'

The downside of the HTD label (and others like Angel Air) is that they tend to repackage and recycle material, and they also have releases that slip from the shelves with alarming regularity. They also like to license material at the drop of the proverbial (which is an economic necessity, I suppose, to be fair), which is why I have included this. It has no new material but another way of getting your hands on material that may otherwise be elusive.

Where But For Caravan Would I? (Universal 2000)

Disc I:
'Place of My Own' (mono)
'Love Song With Flute' (mono)
'Magic Man' (mono)
'Where But For Caravan Would I?' (mono)

'A Day In The Life Of Maurice Haylett'
'If I Could Do It All Over Again, I'd Do It All over You'
'And I Wish I Were Stoned / Don't Worry'
'Asforteri 25'
'Golf Girl' (extended version)
'Nine Feet Underground'

Disc 2:
'Winter Wine'
'Love to Love You' (extended version)
'The Love In Your Eye'
'Memory Lain, Hugh / Headloss'
'L'Auberge du Sanglier / A Hunting We Shall go / Pengola / Backwards / A Hunting We Shall Go (Reprise)'
'Mirror For The Day'
'The Show of Our Lives'
'Stuck In A Hole' (single version)
'No Backstage Pass'
'For Richard' (live)

If you had a young person approach you and ask 'daddy, what were Caravan like?' then you could hand them this and tell them that it's a good indication of what drove the old man mad with joy back in the day. Nothing of note on here, but a good selection. Obviously, as a Universal product it has nothing post-*Cunning Stunts*, and for someone who thinks there could be a good 1976-82 anthology in the BTM and Kingdom years, it lacks somewhat. Nice package, though, if more in tune with Universal's general reaping of the Decca/Deram archives at the time than being very 'Caravan'.

The World Is Yours: A Caravan Anthology 1968-76 (Deram 2010)
Disc: 1
'Place Of My Own' (Stereo Version)
'Magic Man' (Stereo Version)
'Love Song With Flute' (Stereo Version)
'Grandma's Lawn' (Stereo Version)
'Cecil Rons' (Stereo Version)
'Where But For Caravan Would I?' (Stereo Version)
'A Day In The Life Of Maurice Haylett'
'If I Could Do It All Over Again, I'd Do It All Over You'
'Hello, Hello' (Demo Version)
'And I Wish I Were Stoned / Don't Worry'
'Asforteri'
'Can't Be Long Now'
'With An Ear To The Ground You Can Make It'

Disc: 2
'Golf Girl'
'In The Land Of Grey And Pink'
'Nine Feet Underground' (Medley)
'Winter Wine'
'I Don't Know It's Name' (Alias The Word)
'Love To Love You' (BBC Session – Sounds Of The Seventies 11/03/71)
'Feelin', Reelin', Squealin'' (BBC Live – John Peel's Sunday Concert 06/05/71)
'The Love In Your Eye' (First Version)
'The World Is Yours'
'Aristocracy'

Disc: 3
'Waterloo Lily'
'Any Advance On Carpet'
'C'thlu Thlu'
'Memory Lain, Hugh / Headloss'
'The Dog, The Dog, He's At It Again'
'L'Auberge Du Sanglier / A Hunting We Shall Go / Pengola / Backwards / A Hunting We Shall Go'
'Mirror For The Day' (Live At The Theatre Royal, Drury Lane, 28 October, 1973)
'For Richard' (Live At The Theatre Royal, Drury Lane, 28 October, 1973)
'Virgin On The Ridiculous' (Live At The Fairfield Halls)

Disc: 4
'Be Alright / Chance Of A Lifetime' (Live At The Fairfield Halls)
'The Show Of Our Lives'
'Keeping Back My Love'
'No Backstage Pass'
'Stuck In A Hole'
'The Love In Your Eye' (BBC Session – John Peel 07/02/74)
'The Dabsong Conshirtoe' (BBC In Concert, Paris Theatre – 21/03/75)
'Here I Am'
'A Very Smelly Grubby Oik / Bobbing Wide'
'All The Way ((including John Wayne's single-handed Liberation of Paris)'

In truth, there is nothing new on this box, although if you haven't managed to collect all the remastered and reissued CD's and so have missed out on all the extra tracks, this is a pretty easy (if expensive) way of picking them up. Like any of these releases, it's the package itself that would be of interest to the serious Caravan collector. It's a useful primer for younger listeners (assuming they exist in any number), but the previous anthology, if tracked down second hand, might be a better starting point.

Would you like to write for Sonicbond Publishing?

We are mainly a music publisher, but we also occasionally publish in other genres including film and television. At Sonicbond Publishing we are always on the look-out for authors, particularly for our two main series, On Track and Decades.

Mixing fact with in depth analysis, the On Track series examines the entire recorded work of a particular musical artist or group. All genres are considered from easy listening and jazz to 60s soul to 90s pop, via rock and metal.

The Decades series singles out a particular decade in an artist or group's history and focuses on that decade in more detail than may be allowed in the On Track series.

While professional writing experience would, of course, be an advantage, the most important qualification is to have real enthusiasm and knowledge of your subject. First-time authors are welcomed, but the ability to write well in English is essential.

Sonicbond Publishing has distribution throughout Europe and North America, and all our books are also published in E-book form. Authors will be paid a royalty based on sales of their book. Further details about our books are available from www.sonicbondpublishing.com. To contact us, complete the contact form there or email info@sonicbondpublishing.co.uk